ESSENTIAL TECHNIQUE
FOR BAND

INTERMEDIATE TO ADVANCED STUDIES

T0195173

TIM LAUTZENHEISER

JOHN HIGGINS

CHARLES MENGHINI

PAUL LAVENDER

TOM C. RHODES

DON BIERSCHENK

Percussion consultant and editor
WILL RAPP

To create an account, visit:
www.essentialelementsinteractive.com

Student Activation Code
"E3PC-5772-5397-5737"

ISBN 978-0-634-04423-6

HAL•LEONARD®
CORPORATION
7777 W. BLUEMOUND RD. P.O. BOX 13819 MILWAUKEE, WI 53213

B♭ MAJOR

1. SCALE AND ARPEGGIO

2. EXERCISE IN THIRDS

3. ARPEGGIO STUDY

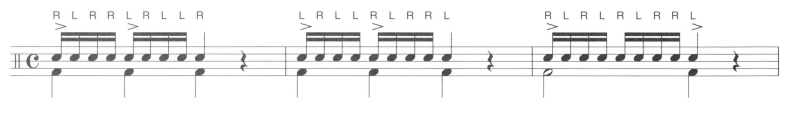

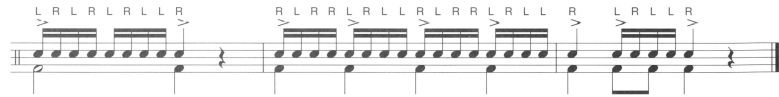

4. TWO-PART ETUDE

5. CHROMATIC SCALE

6. BALANCE BUILDER

6. BALANCE BUILDER – Timpani

divisi or *div.*	Divide the written parts among players, usually into two parts, with equal numbers playing each part.	**THEORY**
unison or *a2*	All players play the same part (usually found after a divisi section).	

7. CHORALE

Tam-Tam (Gong)

Tam-Tam is the name given to a large, flat gong with no definite pitch. While the Gong has a rich history dating back to the early sixth century in China, the Tam-Tam is the specific type of gong that has traditionally been used in western band and orchestra music. Use a heavy mallet designed for this instrument; a concert bass drum mallet is not heavy enough to bring out the low, fundamental sound.

Experiment to find the "sweet spot" on the instrument, typically near the center, where the fundamental sound is best. Until a Tam-Tam starts vibrating, the initial sound is often late. You can compensate for this by "priming" the instrument; that is, lightly tapping the instrument with the mallet two or three times prior to playing your first note.

8. GREAT GATE OF KIEV

Modeste Mussorgsky

8. GREAT GATE OF KIEV – Timpani

Modeste Mussorgsky

THEORY

16th Note Rhythm

This is an excellent review of the eighth-sixteenth note rhythms learned in EE Book 2. Count carefully to ensure rhythmic accuracy.

9. CHILDREN'S SHOES

Black American Spiritual

English composer **George Frideric Handel** (1685–1759) is among the best known composers of the **Baroque Period (1600–1750).** *Sound an Alarm* (from *Judas Maccabaeus*) and his most famous work, the *Hallelujah Chorus,* (from *Messiah*) are two well-known melodies from his **oratorios**, large scale works for solo voices, chorus, and orchestra.

10. SOUND AN ALARM

George Frideric Handel

11. HALLELUJAH CHORUS

George Frideric Handel

12. RHYTHM RAP *Clap the rhythm while counting and tapping.*

THEORY

$\frac{3}{8}$ **Time Signature**   = **3 beats** per measure
= **Eighth** note gets one beat   ♪ = 1 beat   ♩ = 2 beats   ♩. = 3 beats

3/8 time is usually played with a slight emphasis on the 1st beat of each measure. In faster music, this primary beat will make the music feel like it's counted "in 1."

13. RHYTHM RAP *Compare this exercise with No. 12.*

14. WALTZ PETITE

15. MOLLY BANN

English Folksong

$\frac{9}{8}$ Time Signature

$\frac{9}{8}$ = **9 beats** per measure
= **Eighth** note gets one beat

♪ = 1 beat   ♩ = 3 beats
♩ = 2 beats   ♩. = 6 beats

9/8 time is usually played with a slight emphasis on the **1st**, **4th**, and **7th** beats of each measure. This divides the measure into 3 groups of 3 beats each. In faster music, these three primary beats will make the music feel like it's counted "in 3."

16. RHYTHM RAP   *Clap the rhythm while counting and tapping.*

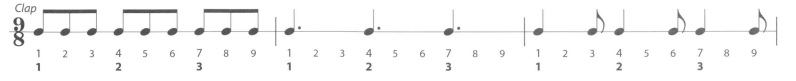

17. SUNDAY AT NINE

Andante

G MINOR

THEORY

Minor Keys

Minor keys and their scales sound different from major keys because of their different pattern of whole and half steps. Each minor key is *relative* or "related" to the major key with the same key signature.

The simplest form of a minor key is called **natural minor**. Two other types are **harmonic minor** and **melodic minor**, each of which have certain altered tones.

18. NATURAL MINOR

19. HARMONIC MINOR

Concert Tom-Toms

Concert Tom-Toms are usually single headed, graduated in size, and mounted on a stand. Hard felt mallets are recommended. The most resonant sound is achieved by playing toward the edge of the head.

20. PAT-A-PAN

French

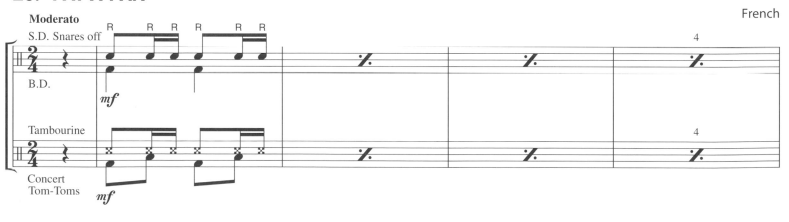

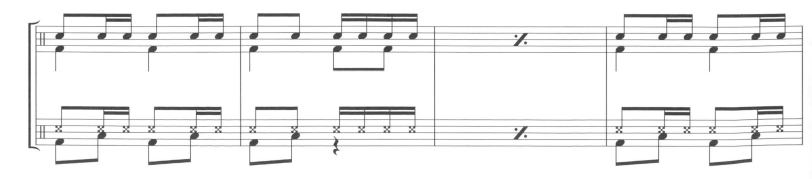

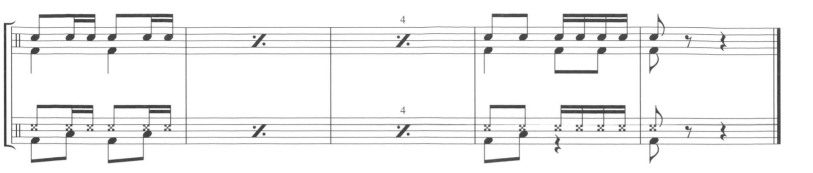

Anvil (Brake Drum)

The metallic sound of a hammer on an anvil (metal block) can be heard in several famous Opera scores of Verdi and Wagner. The most common substitution is the use of an automobile brake drum, which has been used by modern American composers such as John Cage and Lou Harrison. Use a small ball-type hammer or hard bell mallet.

21. THE SLEDGEHAMMER SONG

Russian

22. ESSENTIAL ELEMENTS QUIZ – AUSTRALIAN FOLK SONG

Australian

Eb MAJOR

23. SCALE AND ARPEGGIO

24. EXERCISE IN THIRDS

25. ARPEGGIO STUDY

26. TWO-PART ETUDE

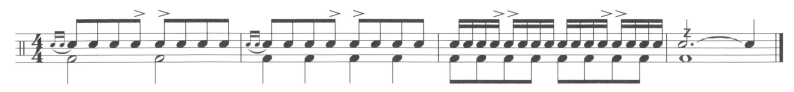

27. CHROMATIC SCALE

28. BALANCE BUILDER

28. BALANCE BUILDER – Timpani

29. CHORALE

HISTORY

Austrian composer **Johann Strauss Jr.** (1825–1899) is also known as "The Waltz King." He wrote some of the world's most famous waltzes (dances in 3/4 meter). This waltz is from *Die Fledermaus* ("The Bat"), Strauss' most famous **operetta**. Operettas were the forerunners of today's musicals, such as *Oklahoma, The Sound Of Music, and The Phantom Of The Opera*.

30. ADELE'S SONG

Johann Strauss Jr.

31. MARINE'S HYMN

32. RHYTHM RAP

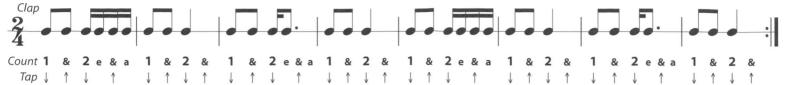

33. KEEPIN' SECRETS

Appalachian Folk Song

34. THE KEEL ROW

Sea Song

⚠ *Count carefully!*

Rudiment
Flam Accent No. 2

This rudiment is a variation of the Flam Accent. Notice that when the rest appears, you omit the sticking that would normally occur if you played at that spot, which produces the double sticking you see in the exercise.

35. JACK'S THE MAN

Moderately

12/8 Time Signature

12/8 = **12 beats** per measure
8 = **Eighth** note gets one beat

♪ = 1 beat   ♩. = 3 beats   ♩. ♩. = 9 beats
♩ = 2 beats   ♩. = 6 beats   𝅝. = 12 beats

12/8 time is usually played with a slight emphasis on the **1st**, **4th**, **7th** and **10th** beats of each measure. This divides the measure into 4 groups of 3 beats each. These four primary beats will make the music feel like it's counted "in 4."

36. RHYTHM RAP *Clap the rhythm while counting and tapping.*

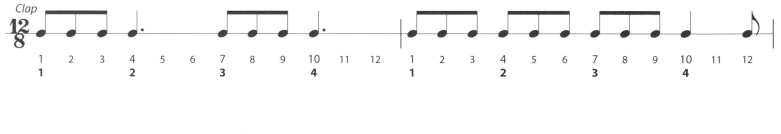

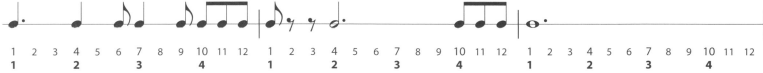

37. SERENADE

38. WITH THINE EYES

molto. rit.

▲ molto - "much"

C MINOR

39. NATURAL MINOR

40. HARMONIC MINOR

HISTORY

Even today, **Native American Indian music** continues to be an important part of tribal dancing ceremonies, using Apache fiddles, rattles, flutes, and log drums to accompany simple songs. American composer **Charles Wakefield Cadman** (1881–1946) wrote this song in 1914 based on Indian melodies he researched throughout his lifetime.

41. SONG OF THE WEEPING SPIRIT

Native American Indian Melody
Adapt. Charles Wakefield Cadman

Lento mysterioso ◀ *Slowly and mysteriously*

42. SCOTTISH LEGEND

Amy Marcy Beach

43. ESSENTIAL ELEMENTS QUIZ *Which measures sound major and which ones minor?*

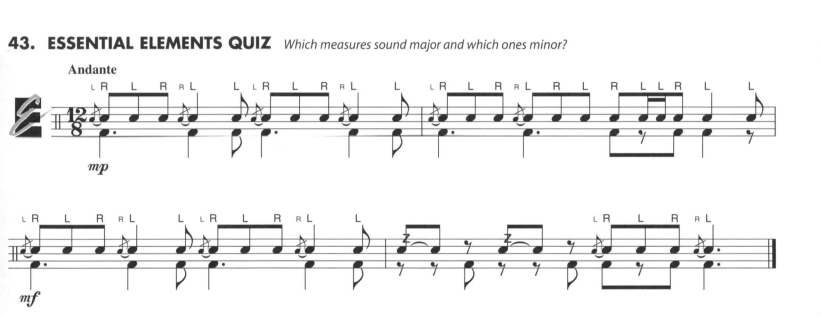

F MAJOR

44. SCALE AND ARPEGGIO

45. EXERCISE IN THIRDS

Rudiment
Reverse Paradiddle

This is one of three variations of the Paradiddle. Notice that the sticking is identical to the Paradiddle, but the accent has been shifted to the third note of each group. This reverses both the feel and sound of the rudiment.

46. ARPEGGIO STUDY

47. TWO-PART ETUDE

48. CHROMATIC SCALE

49. BALANCE BUILDER

49. BALANCE BUILDER – Timpani

50. CHORALE

51. REST ALERT

52. RHYTHM RAP

1 & 2 & 1 e & a 2 & 1 & 2 & 1 e & a 2 & 1 & 2 e & a 1 & 2 e & a 1 e & a 2 & 1 e & a 2 &

53. ISLAND SONG

French composer **Claude Debussy** (1862–1918) created moods and "impressions" with his music. While earlier composers used music to describe events (such as Tchaikovsky's *1812 Overture)*, Debussy's new ideas helped shape today's music. The style of art and music created in this time is called "impressionism." The first automobile was produced during Debussy's lifetime. He died the same year that World War I ended.

54. THE LITTLE CHILD

Claude Debussy

Triplets with Rests

Triplets that start or end with a rest are usually marked with a bracket

55. TRIPLET AND REST VARIATIONS

56. TURKEY IN THE STRAW

American Folk Song

57. ESSENTIAL ELEMENTS QUIZ *Write the first 2 lines of exercise 56 in cut time.*

Sixteenth Notes and Rests
in $\frac{6}{8}, \frac{3}{8}, \frac{9}{8}, \frac{12}{8}$

♬ = ½ beat   ♦ = ½ beat   ♩ = 2 beats   ♭ = 2 beats
♪ = 1 beat   ♦ = 1 beat   ♩· = 3 beats   ♭· = 3 beats

58. RHYTHM RAP

59. SONATINA

D MINOR

60. NATURAL MINOR

61. HARMONIC MINOR

62. COSSACK MARCH

63. SLAVONIC DANCE NO. 2

Antonin Dvořák

64. ESSENTIAL ELEMENTS QUIZ – THE PRETTY GIRL

Irish

A♭ MAJOR

Rudiment
Four Stroke Ruff

This is the traditional name given to the rudiment now called the Single Stroke Four (see Snare Drum International Rudiments section, courtesy of the Percussive Arts Society page 45). While the Single Stoke Four best describes how this rudiment is used in marching percussion applications, the Four Stroke Ruff (traditional name) is the term when the rudiment is used in a concert or orchestral application.

The same alternate sticking R L R L (or L R L R) should be used to learn this rudiment. Care should be taken to play all of the grace notes ahead of the beat to keep all rhythms accurate.

65. SCALE AND ARPEGGIO

66. EXERCISE IN THIRDS

67. ARPEGGIO STUDY

68. TWO-PART ETUDE

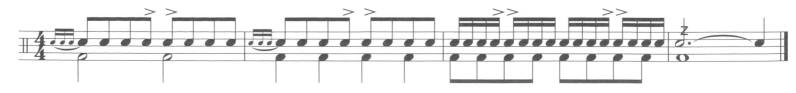

69. CHROMATIC SCALE

70. BALANCE BUILDER

70. BALANCE BUILDER – Timpani

71. CHORALE

HISTORY

The Star Spangled Banner is the national anthem of the United States of America. Francis Scott Key wrote the words during the 1814 battle at Fort McHenry. He listened to the sounds of the fighting throughout the night while being detained on a ship. At dawn, he saw the American flag still flying over the fort. He was inspired to write these words, which were later set to the melody of a popular English song.

72. THE STAR SPANGLED BANNER

Words by Francis Scott Key
Music by John Stafford Smith

Dynamics

pp – *pianissimo* (play very softly)   *ff* – *fortissimo* (play very loudly)

Remember to use full breath support to produce the best possible tone and intonation.

73. INTERMEZZO

Tambourine - Thumb Rolls

74. RHYTHM RAP

75. MORNING STAR

76. SONATA

Wolfgang Amadeus Mozart

77. RONDEAU

Jean-Joseph Mouret

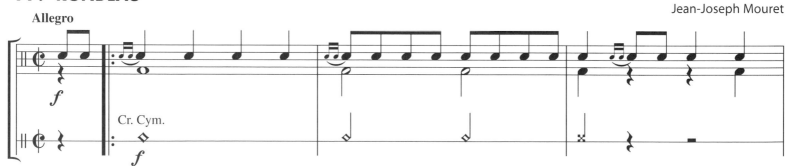

77. RONDEAU – Timpani

Allegro

Jean-Joseph Mouret

Grace Note ♪ A small note (or notes) which is played on, or slightly before the beat.

THEORY

78. JULIET'S WALTZ

Tempo di valse

Charles Gounod

F MINOR

79. NATURAL MINOR

80. HARMONIC MINOR

81. SORCERER'S APPRENTICE

Paul Dukas

Allegro agitato ◁ *Agitated*

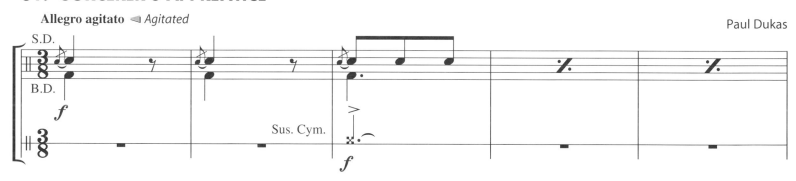

Brushes Brushes with wire strands are recommended for the exercises in this book. Using a counterclockwise motion, the left hand should make a complete circle on each beat (stems down), while the right hand plays the rhythm (stems up).

82. I WALK THE ROAD AGAIN

American

Brushes: Left hand swish, Right hand plays rhythm

83. ESSENTIAL ELEMENTS QUIZ – GREENSLEEVES

English Folk Song

Andante

C MAJOR

84. SCALE AND ARPEGGIO

85. EXERCISE IN THIRDS

Rudiment
Inward Paradiddle

This is one of three variations of the Paradiddle. Notice that the sticking is identical to the Paradiddle, but the accent has been shifted to the fourth sixteenth note of each group, placing this paradiddle variation on the inside of the beat.

86. ARPEGGIO STUDY

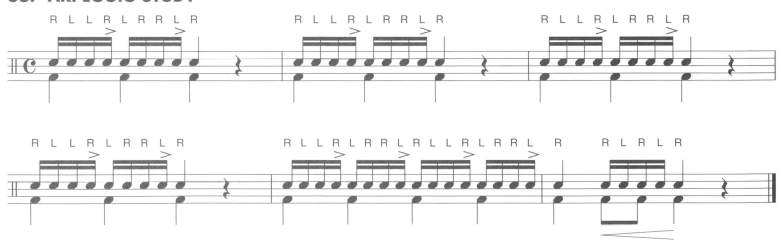

87. TWO-PART ETUDE

88. CHROMATIC SCALE

89. BALANCE BUILDER

89. BALANCE BUILDER – Timpani

90. CHORALE

HISTORY

Black American spirituals originated in the 1700's. As one of the largest categories of true American folk music, these melodies were sung and passed on for generations without being written down. Black and white people worked together to publish the first spiritual collection in 1867, four years after *The Emancipation Proclamation* was signed into law.

91. SIT DOWN, SISTER

Allegro

Black American Spiritual

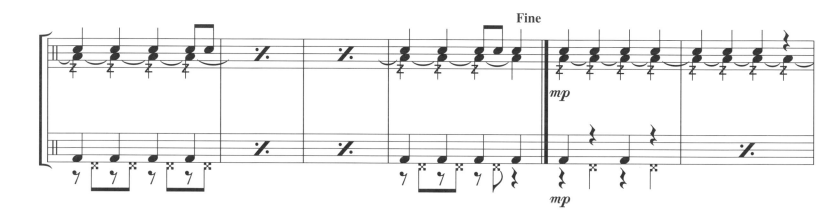

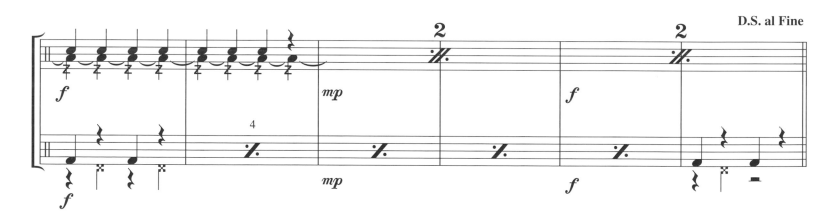

92. SPINNING SONG – Duet

Johann Ellmenreich

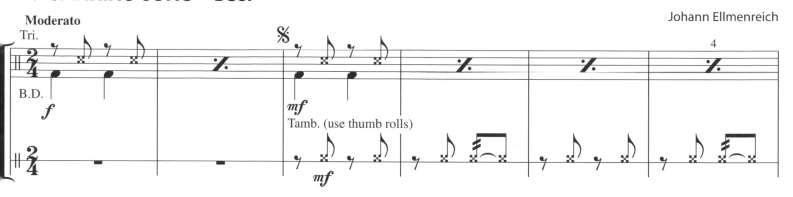

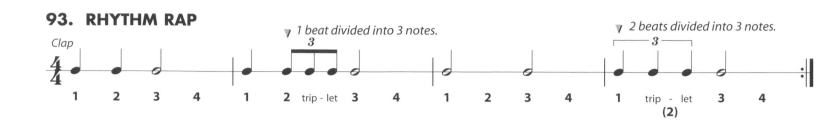

THEORY

Quarter Note Triplets

Similar to eighth note triplets where 1 beat is divided into 3 equal notes, quarter note triplets divide 2 beats into 3 equal notes.

93. RHYTHM RAP

94. THREE FOR TWO

95. SURIRAM'S SONG

Malaysian Folk Song

Africa is a large continent that is made up of many nations, and **African folk music** is as diverse as its many cultures. Folk songs from any country are expressions of work, love, war, sadness and joy. This song is from Tanzania. The words describe a rabbit hopping and running through a field. Listen to the percussion section play African-sounding drums and rhythms.

Agogo Bells   Traditionally an Iron Double Bell of African origin (with two pitches), the modern Agogo Bell is from Brazil, somewhat smaller in size, and made of steel. Use a stick and play toward the open end of each bell. If not available, substitute two different size cowbells.

96. JIBULI (The Rabbit's Song)

Allegro   Adapted Tanzanian Folk Song
Congas and Agogo Bells *a2*

A MINOR

97. NATURAL MINOR

98. HARMONIC MINOR

Meter Changes

Meter changes, or changing time signatures within a section of music, are commonly found in contemporary music. Composers use this technique to create a unique rhythm, pulse, or musical style.

99. TIME ZONES

Important French composers of the late 19th century include **Claude Debussy** (1862–1918), **Gabriel Fauré** (1845–1924), **Erik Satie** (1866–1925), **César Franck** (1822–1890), **Camille Saint-Saëns** (1835–1921), and **Paul Dukas** (1865–1935). Their works continue to have influence on the music of modern day composers. Gabriel Fauré wrote *Pavanne* (originally for orchestra) in 1887, two years before the Eiffel Tower was completed in Paris.

Finger Cymbals

These small brass cymbals should be played by holding the edges perpendicular (at a right angle) to one another, then lightly striking the edges together. In the case of the heavier, cast cymbals, some performers prefer allow both cymbals to hang, then drop one past other, allowing the edges to come in contact. Experiment to achieve the best sound.

100. PAVANNE

Andante espressivo

Gabriel Fauré

D♭ MAJOR

Rudiment

Four Stroke Ruff

Now that you have established the alternate sticking pattern used to play the graces notes ahead of the beat, begin to practice controlled bounces with **both hands together** (Example 1). Once you gain a level of comfort, begin to move one hand just slightly ahead of the other each time you begin a set of controlled bounces. As soon as you get one hand to move slightly ahead of the other, you will immediately hear the four notes articulated clearly (Example 2). This is an alternative approach to using four fast single strokes when playing the Four Stroke Ruff.

101. SCALE AND ARPEGGIO

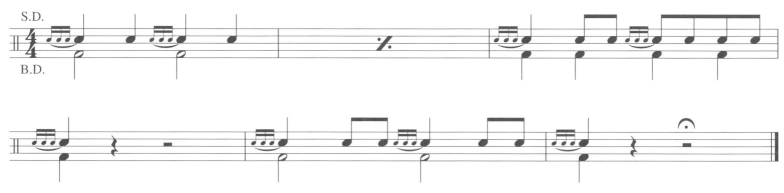

102. EXERCISE IN THIRDS

103. ARPEGGIO STUDY

104. TWO-PART ETUDE

105. CHROMATIC SCALE

106. BALANCE BUILDER

Sus. Cym.

106. BALANCE BUILDER – Timpani

107. CHORALE

Andante

Triangle

mf

rit.

108. GERMAN NATIONAL ANTHEM

Franz Josef Haydn

Maestoso *Five and Nine Stroke Roll Review*

109. JOY

Johann Sebastian Bach

Andante espressivo ◁ *Expressively*

$\frac{5}{4}$ Time Signature

$\frac{5}{4}$ = **5 beats** per measure
= **Quarter** note gets one beat

Conducting

Practice conducting these five-beat patterns.

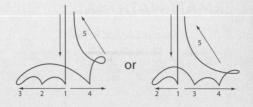

or

110. RHYTHM RAP

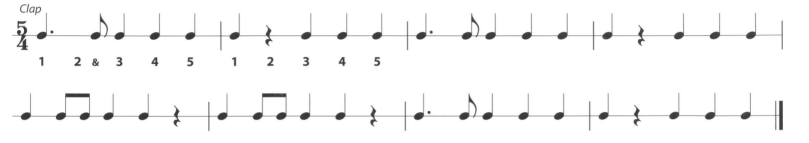

Clap

1   2   &   3   4   5   1   2   3   4   5

111. LET'S COUNT FIVE

Moderato

S.D.

B.D.

mf

sfz

112. SUKURU ITO

Moderato

African Folk Song

Snares off

mf

HISTORY

English composer **George Frideric Handel** (1685–1759) lived during the **Baroque Period (1600–1750)**. *Water Music* was written in honor of England's King George I. The first performance took place on the Thames River on July 17, 1717. Fifty musicians performed the work while floating on a barge. Handel lived during the same time as Johann Sebastian Bach, perhaps the most famous Baroque composer.

113. WATER MUSIC

Allegro maestoso

George Frideric Handel

f

113. WATER MUSIC – Timpani

Allegro maestoso

George Frideric Handel

f

f

114. ESSENTIAL TECHNIQUE QUIZ – PICTURES AT AN EXHIBITION

Modeste Mussorgsky

B♭ MINOR

115. NATURAL MINOR

116. HARMONIC MINOR

Ostinato

A clear and distinct musical phrase that is repeated persistently.

British composer **Gustav Holst** (1874–1934) is one of the most widely played composers for concert band today. Many of his compositions, including his familiar military suites, are based on tuneful English folk songs. His most famous work for orchestra, *The Planets (1916),* has seven movements—one written for each known planet, excluding Earth. At this time, Pluto was undiscovered.

117. MARS – Duet/Trio

Energetico ◁ *With energy*

Gustav Holst

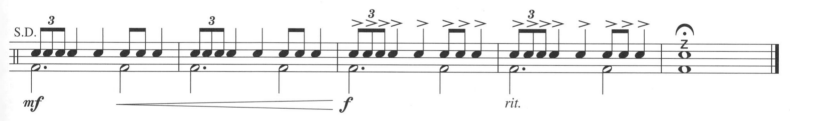

117. MARS – Duet/Trio – Timpani

Gustav Holst

G MAJOR

118. SCALE AND ARPEGGIO

119. EXERCISE IN THIRDS

Tap Flam Review

Rudiment

Delayed Paradiddle

This is one of three variations of the Paradiddle. Notice that the sticking is identical to the Paradiddle, but the accent has been shifted (or delayed) to the second sixteenth note of each group.

120. ARPEGGIO STUDY

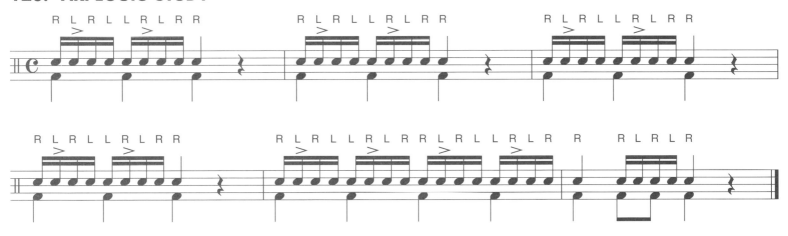

121. TWO-PART ETUDE

Flam Paradiddle Review

122. CHROMATIC SCALE
Pataflafla Review

123. BALANCE BUILDER

123. BALANCE BUILDER – Timpani

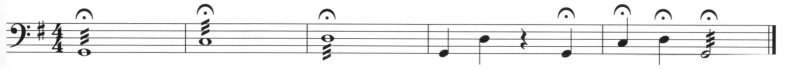

124. CHORALE

Norwegian composer **Edvard Grieg** (1843–1907) based much of his music on the folk songs and dances of Norway. During the late 19th century, composers often used melodies from their native land. This trend is called **nationalism**. Russian **Modeste Mussorgsky** (1839–1881), Czech **Antonin Dvořák** (1841–1904), and Englishman **Sir Edward Elgar** (1857–1934) are other famous composers whose music was influenced by nationalism.

Rudiment
Crushed Ruff

Essentially, the Crushed Ruff is one of the easiest drum rudiments to master. Simply play a multiple bounce stroke with both hands at the same time.

125. NORWEGIAN DANCE

Edvard Grieg

126. FRENCH NATIONAL ANTHEM (LA MARSEILLAISE)

Rouget De L'Isle

Music written during the **Renaissance Period (1430–1600)** was often upbeat and dance-like. *Wolsey's Wilde* was originally written for the lute, an ancestor to the guitar and the most popular instrument of the Renaissance era. Modern day concert band composer Gordon Jacob used this popular song in his *William Byrd Suite,* written as a tribute to English composer William Byrd (1543–1623).

HISTORY

127. WOLSEY'S WILDE

Animato ◁ *Animated, lively*

Anonymous

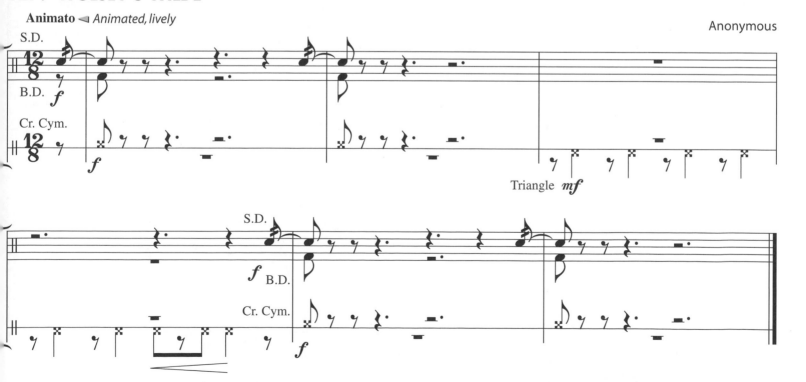

E MINOR

128. NATURAL MINOR

129. HARMONIC MINOR

HISTORY

Native Japanese instruments include the *shakuhachi,* a bamboo flute played pointing downward; the *koto,* a long zither with movable frets played sitting down; and the *gakubiwa,* a pear-shaped lute with strings that are plucked. These instruments have been an important part of Japanese culture since the 8th century. *Kabuki,* a Japanese theatrical form that originated in 1603, remains popular in Japan. Performers play native Japanese instruments during Kabuki performances.

130. SONG OF THE SHAKUHACHI

Japanese Folk Song

Andante
Temple Blocks

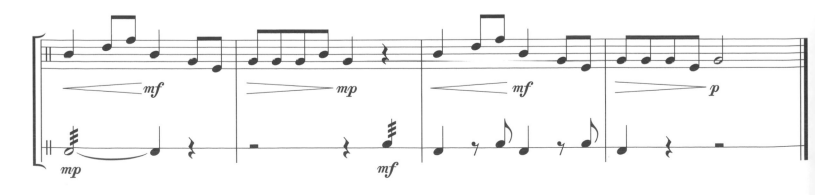

| **D.C. al Coda** | At the **D.C. al Coda**, play again from the beginning to the indication **To Coda ⊕**, then skip to the section marked **⊕ Coda**, meaning "ending section." |
| **D.S. al Coda** | Similar to **D.C. al Coda**, but return to the sign 𝄋. |

131. POLOVETZIAN DANCES

Alexander Borodin

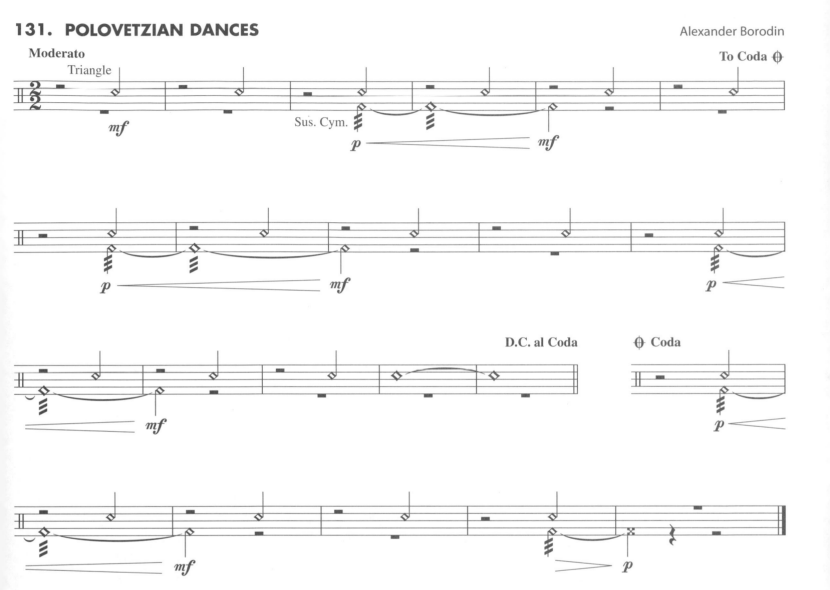

D MAJOR

132. SCALE AND ARPEGGIO

133. EXERCISE IN THIRDS

Rudiment
Thirteen Stroke Roll

Use open, double bounces to play thirteen evenly divided notes in order to form this measured roll. Remember that the hands will be moving at the speed of sixteenth notes. The Thirteen Stroke Roll starts on the beat and ends on next upbeat.

134. ARPEGGIO STUDY

Rudiment
Seventeen Stroke Roll

Use open, double bounces to play seventeen evenly divided notes in order to form this measured roll. Remember that the hands will be moving at the speed of sixteenth notes; the double bounces will sound the correct thirty-second note rhythm.

135. TWO-PART ETUDE

136. CHORALE

Andante
Sus. Cym.

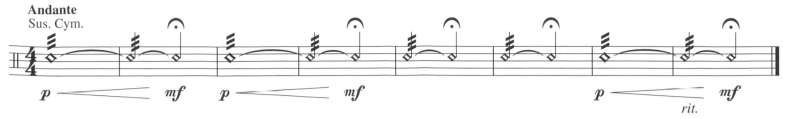

B MINOR

137. NATURAL MINOR

138. HARMONIC MINOR

Latin American Music combines the folk music from South and Central America, the Carribean Islands, American Indian, Spanish and Portuguese cultures. Melodies are often accompanied by drums, maracas, and claves. Latin American music continues to influence jazz, classical, and popular styles of music. *Cielito Lindo* is a Latin American love song.

139. CIELITO LINDO

C. Fernandez

Tchaikovsky, along with Wagner, Brahms, Mendelssohn, and Chopin, helped define the musical era known as the **Romantic Period (1825–1900)**. The "symphonic tone poem" from this period continues to be one of the most popular musical forms performed by orchestras and bands today.

140. WALTZ IN FIVE (from SYMPHONY NO. 6)

Peter I. Tchaikovsky

141. THE YOUNG CHEVALIER

Scottish

Sticking Exercise

G♭ MAJOR

142. SCALE AND ARPEGGIO

Seven Stroke Roll

Use open, double bounces to play seven evenly divided notes in order to form this measured roll. Remember that the hands will be moving at the speed of sixteenth notes. The Seven Stroke Roll in this exercise starts on the beat and ends on the sixteenth note preceding the next beat. The exact notation for this roll can be found in the Snare Drum International Drum Rudiments section of the book.

143. EXERCISE IN THIRDS

144. ARPEGGIO STUDY

Seven/Seventeen Stroke Roll Combination

145. TWO-PART ETUDE

Seventeen/Nine Stroke Roll Combination

146. CHORALE

Andante

Sus. Cym.

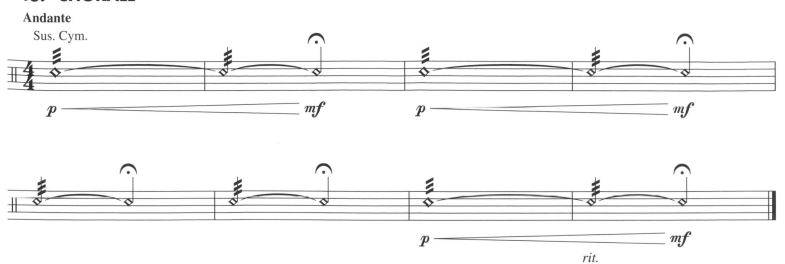

E♭ MINOR

147. NATURAL MINOR

Extended Roll Exercise

148. HARMONIC MINOR

Variation - Extended Roll Exercise

INDIVIDUAL STUDY – Percussion

149. SINGLE PARADIDDLE VARIATIONS

Slow – CD Track 2
Fast – CD Track 3

150. SINGLE PARADIDDLE/REVERSE PARADIDDLE EXERCISE

Slow – CD Track 4
Fast – CD Track 5

151. TRIPLE/DOUBLE/SINGLE PARADIDDLE COMBINATION

Slow – CD Track 6
Fast – CD Track 7

INDIVIDUAL STUDY – Percussion

Slow – CD Track 8
Fast – CD Track 9

152. SINGLE PARADIDDLE/SINGLE STROKE FOUR COMBINATION

Slow – CD Track 10
Fast – CD Track 11

153. SINGLE PARADIDDLE/SINGLE STROKE FOUR VARIATION

INDIVIDUAL STUDY – Percussion

Drag Paradiddle No. 1

This new rudiment combines a Single Drag with a Paradiddle. It is suggested that you space the grace notes of the Drag evenly in order to maintain consistency in the rhythm.

154. DRAG PARADIDDLE EXERCISE #1

Slow – CD Track 12
Fast – CD Track 13

Drag Paradiddle No. 2

This new rudiment combines a Double Drag with a Paradiddle. Again, it is suggested that you space the grace notes of the Drag evenly in order to maintain consistency in the rhythm.

Lesson 25

This is the reverse of the rudiment presented in the Snare Drum International Drum Rudiments (courtesy of the Percussive Arts Society), but it is the pattern most often encountered in concert or orchestral music. Similar to the concept used in the Drag Paradiddle rudiments, it is suggested that you space the notes of the Drag evenly in order to maintain consistency in the rhythm.

155. DRAG PARADIDDLE EXERCISE #2 – Rat-a-Tap Combinations

Slow – CD Track 14
Fast – CD Track 15

INDIVIDUAL STUDY – Percussion

Single Ratamacue

Similar to the concept used in the Drag Paradiddle rudiments, it is suggested that you space the grace notes evenly in order to maintain consistency in the rhythm.

156. SINGLE RATAMACUE EXERCISE

Slow – CD Track 16
Fast – CD Track 17

Triple Ratamacue

Similar to the concept used in the Drag Paradiddle rudiments, it is suggested that you space the grace notes evenly in order to maintain consistency in the rhythm.

157. TRIPLE RATAMACUE/SINGLE RATAMACUE COMBINATION

Slow – CD Track 18
Fast – CD Track 19

READING SKILL BUILDERS

158. READING SKILL BUILDER NO. 1 *CD Track 20*

159. READING SKILL BUILDER NO. 2 *CD Track 21*

EA--IN SKILL B IL--E S

160. READING SKILL BUILDER NO. 3

CD Track 22

161. READING SKILL BUILDER NO. 4

CD Track 23

162. READING SKILL BUILDER NO. 5

CD Track 24

READING SKILL BUILDERS

163. READING SKILL BUILDER NO. 6

CD Track 25

164. READING SKILL BUILDER NO. 7

CD Track 26

READING SKILL BUILDERS

165. READING SKILL BUILDER NO. 8

CD Track 27

166. READING SKILL BUILDER NO. 9

CD Track 28

167. CHORALE (Prelude from Hansel and Gretel) *CD Track 29*

Engelbert Humperdinck
Arr. by John Higgins

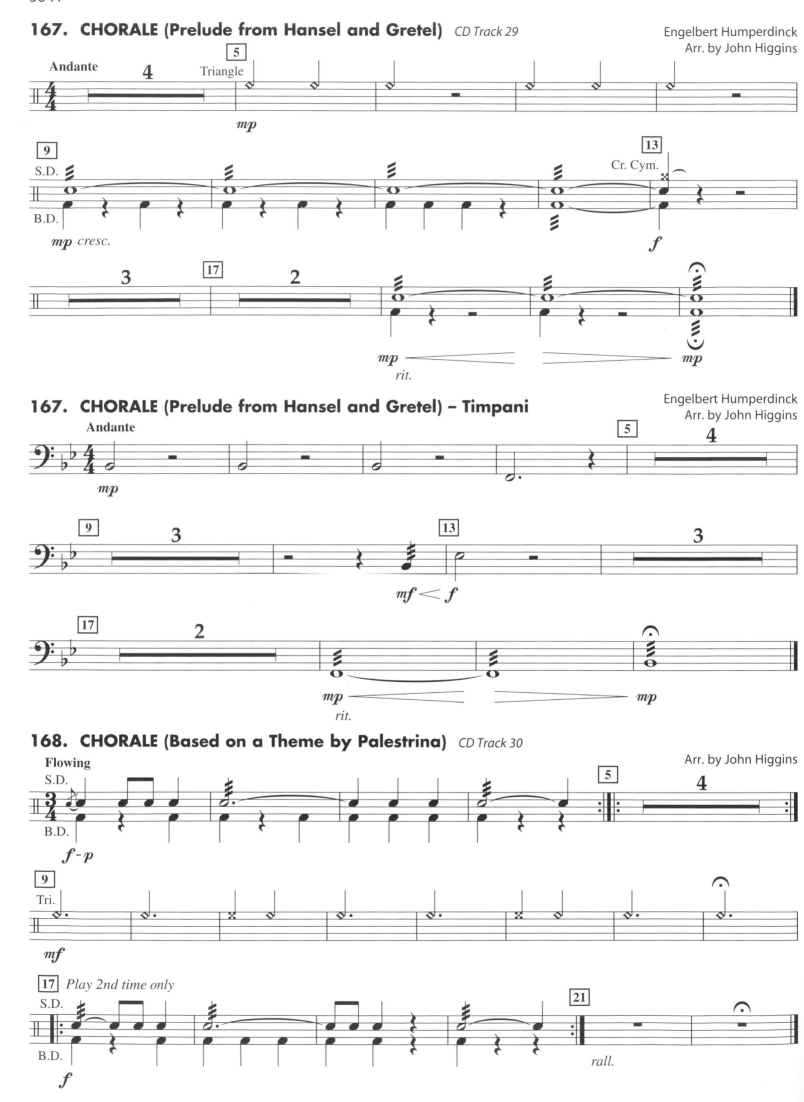

167. CHORALE (Prelude from Hansel and Gretel) – Timpani

Engelbert Humperdinck
Arr. by John Higgins

168. CHORALE (Based on a Theme by Palestrina) *CD Track 30*

Arr. by John Higgins

168. CHORALE (Based on a Theme by Palestrina) – Timpani

Arr. by John Higgins

170. CHORALE (Based on a Theme by Tchaikovsky) *CD Track 32*

Arr. by John Higgins

172. CHORALE (Navy Hymn) *CD Track 34*

John Dykes
Arr. by John Higgins

172. CHORALE (Navy Hymn) – Timpani

John Dykes
Arr. by John Higgins

173. CHORALE (Prelude) *CD Track 35*

Frederic Chopin
Arr. by John Higgins

173. CHORALE (Prelude) – Timpani

Frederic Chopin
Arr. by John Higgins

RHYTHM STUDIES

CD Tracks 27–28

CD Tracks 29–30

CD Tracks 31–32

CD Tracks 33–34

CD Tracks 35–36

RHYTHM STUDIES

CD Tracks 37–38

CD Tracks 39–40

CD Tracks 41–42

CD Tracks 43–44

CD Tracks 45–46

THE BASICS OF JAZZ STYLE from Essential Elements for Jazz Ensemble

Accenting "2 and 4"

For most traditional music the important beats in 4/4 time are 1 and 3. In jazz, however, the emphasis is usually on beats 2 and 4. Emphasizing "2 and 4" gives the music a jazz feeling.

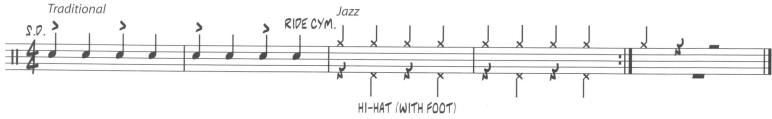

174. ACCENTING 2 AND 4 *CD Track 56*

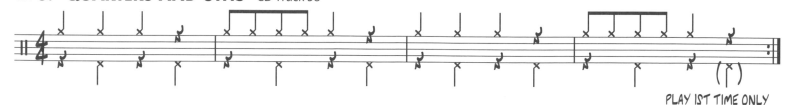

Note: In jazz drumming, accents on 2 and 4 are achieved by adding the hi-hat and/or snare drum.

Jazz Articulations

These are the four basic articulations in jazz.

| **Tenuto**
(full value) | **Staccato**
(short, unaccented) | **Long Accent**
(full value, accented) | **Roof Top Accent**
(short, accented) |

Swing 8th Notes Sound Different Than They Look

In swing, the 2nd 8th note of each beat is actually played like the last third of a triplet, and slightly accented. 8th notes in swing style are usually played legato.

175. SWING 8TH NOTES *CD Track 57*

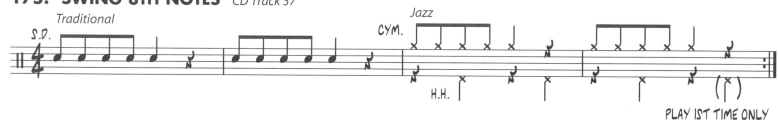

Quarter Notes

Quarter notes in swing style are usually played detached (staccato) with accents on beats 2 and 4.

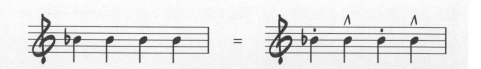

176. QUARTERS AND 8THS *CD Track 58*

177. RUNNIN' AROUND *CD Track 59*

Syncopation in Jazz

When beats are played early (anticipated) or played late (delayed),
the music becomes syncopated. Syncopation makes the music sound "jazzy."

178. WHEN THE SAINTS GO MARCHING IN – Without Syncopation *CD Track 60*

James Black and Katherine Purvis

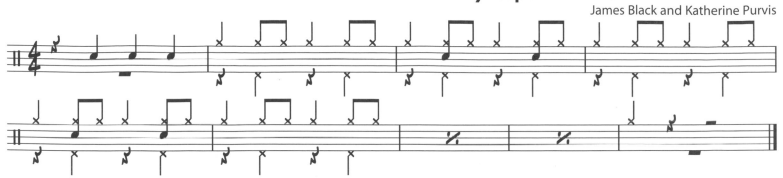

179. WHEN THE SAINTS GO MARCHING IN – With Syncopation *CD Track 61*

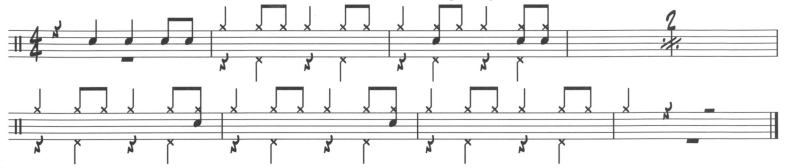

"Jazzin' Up" the Melody by Adding Rhythms

Adding rhythms to a melody is another easy way to improvise in a jazz style. Start by filling out long notes with
repeated 8th and quarter notes. Remember to swing the 8th notes (play legato and give the upbeats an accent).

180. "JAZZIN' UP" JINGLE BELLS *CD Track 62*

Original Melody

J. Pierpont

Jazzed Up Melody (rhythms added)

181. LONDON BRIDGE – MAKE UP YOUR OWN (IMPROVISE) *CD Track 63*

Original Melody

Jazzed Up Melody

THEORY

Major Scales

The following patterns have been created to serve as part of your daily practice routine. Play at various dynamic levels and tempos. If you perform any of these exercises with the full band, you may hear different articulation patterns, such as:

182. B♭ MAJOR

Paradiddle Review

CD Track 64

183. E♭ MAJOR

Triple Paradiddle Review

CD Track 65

184. F MAJOR
Double Paradiddle Review

CD Track 66

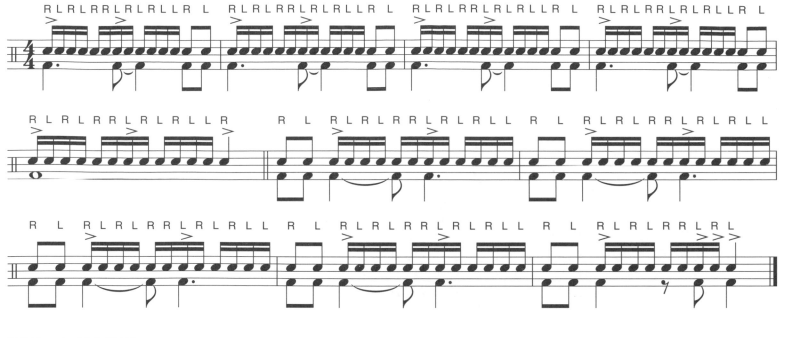

185. C MAJOR
Flamacue Review

CD Track 67

186. A♭ MAJOR
Flam Tap Review

CD Track 68

187. D♭ MAJOR
Flam Paradiddle Review

CD Track 69

188. G MAJOR
Flam Accent Review

CD Track 70

189. D MAJOR

Nine Stroke Roll/Flam Exercise

CD Track 71

190. A MAJOR

Nine Stroke Roll/Flam Tap Exercise

CD Track 72

191. G♭ MAJOR

Seventeen Stroke Roll/Flam Exercise

CD Track 73

THEORY

Minor Scales

Play these exercises as part of your daily practice routine. Play at various dynamic levels and tempos. If you perform these exercises with the full band, you may hear different articulation patterns, such as:

192. D MINOR SCALE
Six Stroke Roll Development Exercise

CD Track 74

193. G MINOR SCALE
Seven Stroke Roll Development Exercise

CD Track 75

194. C MINOR SCALE

Fifteen Stroke Roll Development Exercise

CD Track 76

195. F MINOR SCALE

Extended Roll Development Exercise

CD Track 77

SNARE DRUM INTERNATIONAL DRUM RUDIMENTS

All rudiments should be practiced: open (slow) to close (fast) and/or at an even moderate march tempo.

Instrument Care Reminders

Snare drums occasionally need tuning. Ask your teacher to help you tighten each tension rod equally using a drum key.

- Be careful not to over-tighten the head. It will break if the tension is too tight.
- Loosen the snare strainer at the end of each rehearsal.
- Cover all percussion instruments when not in use.
- Put sticks away in a storage area. Keep the percussion section neat!
- Sticks are the only things which should be placed on the snare drum. NEVER put or allow others to put objects on any percussion instrument.

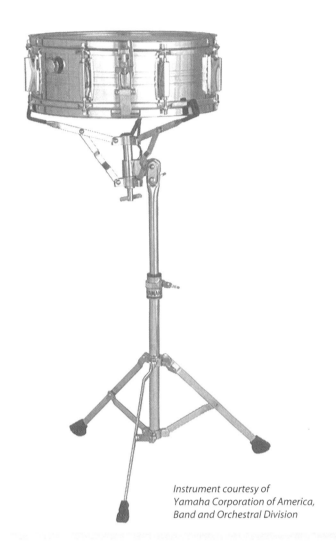

Instrument courtesy of Yamaha Corporation of America, Band and Orchestral Division

I. ROLL RUDIMENTS

A. SINGLE STROKE RUDIMENTS

1. Single Stroke Roll

R L R L R L R L

3. Single Stroke Seven

R L R L R L R
L R L R L R L

2. Single Stroke Four

R L R L   R L R L
L R L R   L R L R

B. MULTIPLE BOUNCE ROLL RUDIMENTS

4. Multiple Bounce Roll

5. Triple Stroke Roll

R R R L L L   R R R L L L

International Drum Rudiments courtesy of the Percussive Arts Society
Copyright © 1984

SNARE DRUM INTERNATIONAL DRUM RUDIMENTS

C. DOUBLE STROKE OPEN ROLL RUDIMENTS

6. Double Stroke Open Roll

R R L L R R L L

7. Five Stroke Roll

R   R   L   L

8. Six Stroke Roll

R   R   L   R
L   R   L

9. Seven Stroke Roll

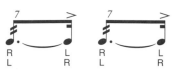
R   L   R   L
L   R   L   R

10. Nine Stroke Roll

R   R   L   L

11. Ten Stroke Roll

R   R L   R   R L
    L R   L R

12. Eleven Stroke Roll

R   R L   R   R L
    L R   L R

13. Thirteen Stroke Roll

R   R   L   L

14. Fifteen Stroke Roll

R   L   R   L
L   R   L   R

15. Seventeen Stroke Roll

R   R   L   L

II. DIDDLE RUDIMENTS

16. Single Paradiddle

R L R R   L R L L

17. Double Paradiddle

R L R L R R   L R L R L L

18. Triple Paradiddle

R L R L R L R R   L R L R L R L L

19. Single Paradiddle-Diddle

R L R R L L   R L R R L L
L R L L R R   L R L L R R

SNARE DRUM INTERNATIONAL DRUM RUDIMENTS

III. FLAM RUDIMENTS

20. Flam

21. Flam Accent

22. Flam Tap

23. Flamacue

24. Flam Paraddile (Flamadiddle)

25. Single Flamed Mill

26. Flam Paradiddle-Diddle

27. Pataflafla

28. Swiss Army Triplet

29. Inverted Flam Tap

30. Flam Drag

IV. DRAG RUDIMENTS

31. Drag

32. Single Drag Tap

33. Double Drag Tap

34. Lesson 25

35. Single Dragadiddle

36. Drag Paradiddle #1

37. Drag Paradiddle #2

38. Single Ratamacue

39. Double Ratamacue

40. Triple Ratamacue

REFERENCE INDEX

Definitions (pg.)

Allegro Agitato 17
Allegro Marziale 27
Allegro Vivo 13
Andante Espressivo 23
Andante Grazioso 16
Animato 27
D.C. al Coda 28
D.S. al Coda 28
Divisi (*div.*) 2
Energetico 25
5/4 23
Fortissimo (*ff*) 15
Giocoso 11
Grace Note 16
Lento 8
Lento Mysterioso 9
Maestoso 3
Meter Changes 21
Minor Keys 5
Molto Rit. 8
9/8 4
Ostinato 25
Quarter Note Triplets 20
Pianissimo (*pp*) 15
16th Notes and Rests
  in 6/8, 3/8, 9/8, 12/8 12
Tempo Di Valse 7
3/8 4
Triplets with Rests 11
12/8 8
Unison (*a2*) 2

Composers

JOHANN SEBASTIAN BACH
• Joy 23

ALEXANDER BORODIN
• Polovetzian Dances 28

CLAUDE DEBUSSY
• The Little Child 11

PAUL DUKAS
• Sorcerer's Apprentice 17

ANTONIN DVORÁK
• Slavonic Dance No. 2 13

JOHANN ELLMENREICH
• Spinning Song 19

GABRIEL FAURÉ
• Pavanne 21

CHARLES GOUNOD
• Juliet's Waltz 16

EDVARD GRIEG
• Norwegian Dance 27

GEORGE FRIDERIC HANDEL
• Hallelujah Chorus 3
• Sound An Alarm 3
• Water Music 24

FRANZ JOSEF HAYDN
• German National Anthem 23

GUSTAV HOLST
• Mars 25

JEAN-JOSEPH MOURET
• Rondeau 16

WOLFGANG AMADEUS MOZART
• Sonata 16

MODESTE MUSSORGSKY
• Great Gate of Kiev 3
• Pictures at an Exhibition 24

JOHANN STRAUSS JR.
• Adele's Song 7

PETER I. TCHAIKOVSKY
• Waltz in Five
  (from Symphony No. 6) 30

World Music

AFRICAN
• Jibuli 20
• Sukuru Ito 24

AMERICAN
• Children's Shoes 3
• I Walk the Road Again 17
• The Keel Row 7
• Keepin' Secrets 7
• Sit Down, Sister 19
• Star Spangled Banner 15
• Turkey in the Straw 12

AUSTRALIAN
• Australian Folk Song 5

ENGLISH
• Greensleeves 17
• Molly Bann 4
• Wolsey's Wilde 27

FRENCH
• Pat-A-Pan 5
• French National Anthem 27

IRISH
• The Pretty Girl 13

JAPANESE
• Song of the Shakuhachi 28

LATIN AMERICAN
• Cielito Lindo 30

MALAYSIAN
• Suriram's Song 20

NATIVE AMERICAN INDIAN
• Song of the Weeping Spirit 9

RUSSIAN
• The Sledgehammer Song 5

SCOTTISH
• Scottish Legend 9
• The Young Chevalier 30

REFERENCE INDEX FOR PERCUSSION

Definitions (pg.)

ESSENTIAL TECHNIQUE
FOR BAND

INTERMEDIATE TO ADVANCED STUDIES

TIM LAUTZENHEISER
JOHN HIGGINS
CHARLES MENGHINI
PAUL LAVENDER
TOM C. RHODES
DON BIERSCHENK
Percussion consultant and editor
WILL RAPP

HAL•LEONARD®
CORPORATION

ESSENTIAL TECHNIQUE
FOR BAND

INTERMEDIATE TO ADVANCED STUDIES

TIM LAUTZENHEISER

JOHN HIGGINS

CHARLES MENGHINI

PAUL LAVENDER

TOM C. RHODES

DON BIERSCHENK

Percussion consultant and editor
WILL RAPP

ISBN 978-0-634-04423-6

7777 W. BLUEMOUND RD. P.O. BOX 13819 MILWAUKEE, WI 53213

B♭ MAJOR

Throughout this book, rolls are for xylophone and marimba only.

1. SCALE AND ARPEGGIO

2. EXERCISE IN THIRDS

3. ARPEGGIO STUDY

4. TWO-PART ETUDE

5. CHROMATIC SCALE

6. BALANCE BUILDER

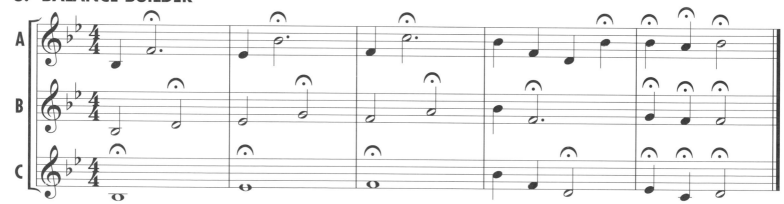

THEORY

divisi or *div.*   Divide the written parts among players, usually into two parts, with equal numbers playing each part.

unison or *a2*   All players play the same part (usually found after a divisi section).

7. CHORALE

8. GREAT GATE OF KIEV

Modeste Mussorgsky

9. CHILDREN'S SHOES

Black American Spiritual

HISTORY

English composer **George Frideric Handel** (1685–1759) is among the best known composers of the **Baroque Period (1600–1750)**. *Sound an Alarm* (from *Judas Maccabaeus*) and his most famous work, the *Hallelujah Chorus,* (from *Messiah*) are two well-known melodies from his **oratorios**, large scale works for solo voices, chorus, and orchestra.

10. SOUND AN ALARM

George Frideric Handel

11. HALLELUJAH CHORUS

George Frideric Handel

4

12. RHYTHM RAP *Clap the rhythm while counting and tapping.*

Clap

3/4
1 2 3 **1** 2 3 **1** 2 3 **1** 2 3 **1** 2 & 3 **1** 2 3 **1** 2 & 3 & **1** 2 3

3/8 Time Signature

  3/8 = **3 beats** per measure
= **Eighth** note gets one beat

♪ = 1 beat   ♩ = 2 beats   ♩. = 3 beats

3/8 time is usually played with a slight emphasis on the 1st beat of each measure. In faster music, this primary beat will make the music feel like it's counted "in 1."

13. RHYTHM RAP *Compare this exercise with No. 12.*

Clap

3/8
1 2 3 **1** 2 3 **1** 2 3 **1** 2 3 **1** 2 & 3 **1** 2 3 **1** 2 & 3 & **1** 2 3

14. WALTZ PETITE

mf

15. MOLLY BANN

English Folksong

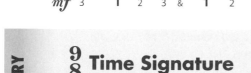 *mf* 3 **1** 2 3 & **1** 2 3   < *f*

9/8 Time Signature

 9/8 = **9 beats** per measure
= **Eighth** note gets one beat

♪ = 1 beat   ♩. = 3 beats
♩ = 2 beats   ♩.. = 6 beats

9/8 time is usually played with a slight emphasis on the **1st**, **4th**, and **7th** beats of each measure. This divides the measure into 3 groups of 3 beats each. In faster music, these three primary beats will make the music feel like it's counted "in 3."

16. RHYTHM RAP *Clap the rhythm while counting and tapping.*

Clap

9/8
1 2 3 4 5 6 7 8 9   1 2 3 4 5 6 7 8 9   1 2 3 4 5 6 7 8 9
1   **2**   **3**   **1**   **2**   **3**   **1**   **2**   **3**

1 2 3 4 5 6 7 8 9   1 2 3 4 5 6 7 8 9   1 2 3 4 5 6 7 8 9   1 2 3 4 5 6 7 8 9
1   **2**   **3**   **1**   **2**   **3**   **1**   **2**   **3**   **1**   **2**   **3**

17. SUNDAY AT NINE

Andante

mf

< *f*

G MINOR

Minor Keys

Minor keys and their scales sound different from major keys because of their different pattern of whole and half steps. Each minor key is *relative* or "related" to the major key with the same key signature.

The simplest form of a minor key is called **natural minor**. Two other types are **harmonic minor** and **melodic minor**, each of which have certain altered tones.

18. NATURAL MINOR *Practice both upper and lower octaves.*

19. HARMONIC MINOR

20. PAT-A-PAN

French

21. THE SLEDGEHAMMER SONG

Russian

22. ESSENTIAL ELEMENTS QUIZ – AUSTRALIAN FOLK SONG

Australian

E♭ MAJOR

23. SCALE AND ARPEGGIO

24. EXERCISE IN THIRDS

25. ARPEGGIO STUDY

26. TWO-PART ETUDE

27. CHROMATIC SCALE

28. BALANCE BUILDER

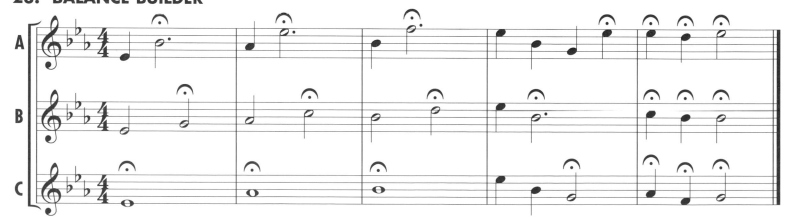

29. CHORALE

HISTORY

Austrian composer **Johann Strauss Jr.** (1825–1899) is also known as "The Waltz King." He wrote some of the world's most famous waltzes (dances in 3/4 meter). This waltz is from *Die Fledermaus* ("The Bat"), Strauss' most famous **operetta**. Operettas were the forerunners of today's musicals, such as *Oklahoma, The Sound Of Music,* and *The Phantom Of The Opera*.

30. ADELE'S SONG

Johann Strauss Jr.

31. MARINE'S HYMN

32. RHYTHM RAP

33. KEEPIN' SECRETS

Appalachian Folk Song

34. THE KEEL ROW

Sea Song

8

35. JACK'S THE MAN

THEORY

$\frac{12}{8}$ **Time Signature**

$\frac{12}{8}$ = **12 beats** per measure
= **Eighth** note gets one beat

♪ = 1 beat   ♩. = 3 beats   ♩.♩. = 9 beats
♩ = 2 beats   ♩. = 6 beats   𝅗𝅥. = 12 beats

12/8 time is usually played with a slight emphasis on the **1st**, **4th**, **7th** and **10th** beats of each measure. This divides the measure into 4 groups of 3 beats each. These four primary beats will make the music feel like it's counted "in 4."

36. RHYTHM RAP   *Clap the rhythm while counting and tapping.*

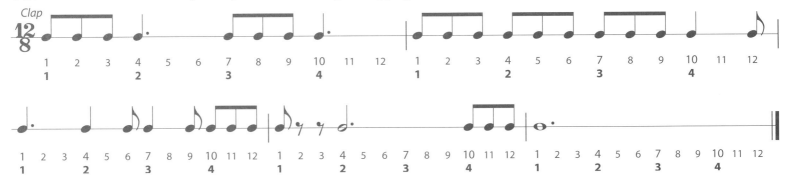

37. SERENADE

38. WITH THINE EYES

molto rit.
△ *molto = "much"*

9

C MINOR

39. NATURAL MINOR

40. HARMONIC MINOR

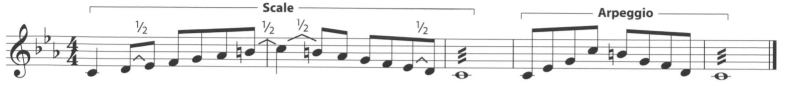

41. SONG OF THE WEEPING SPIRIT

Native American Indian Melody
Adapt. Charles Wakefield Cadman

42. SCOTTISH LEGEND

Amy Marcy Beach

43. ESSENTIAL ELEMENTS QUIZ *Which measures sound major and which ones minor?*

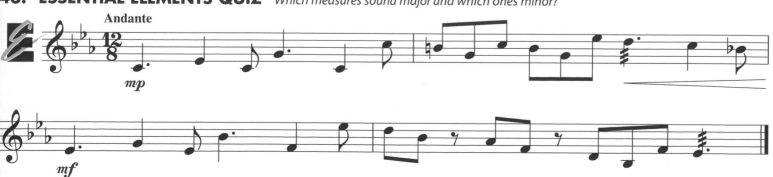

10

F MAJOR

51. REST ALERT

52. RHYTHM RAP

Clap

1 & 2 & 1 e & a 2 & 1 & 2 & 1 e & a 2 & 1 & 2 e & a 1 & 2 e & a 1 e & a 2 & 1 e & a 2 &

53. ISLAND SONG

French composer **Claude Debussy** (1862–1918) created moods and "impressions" with his music. While earlier composers used music to describe events (such as Tchaikovsky's *1812 Overture),* Debussy's new ideas helped shape today's music. The style of art and music created in this time is called "impressionism." The first automobile was produced during Debussy's lifetime. He died the same year that World War I ended.

HISTORY

54. THE LITTLE CHILD

Claude Debussy

Giocoso ◁ *Lightly, happily*

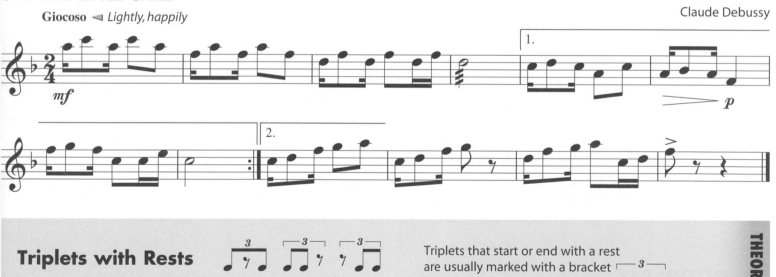

Triplets with Rests

Triplets that start or end with a rest are usually marked with a bracket ⌐—3—

THEORY

55. TRIPLET AND REST VARIATIONS

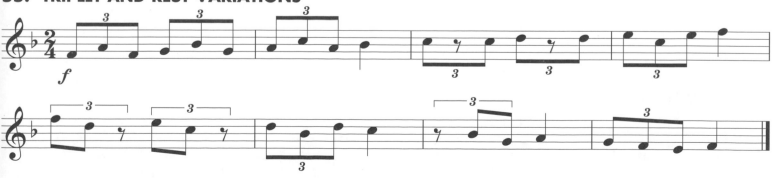

56. TURKEY IN THE STRAW

American Folk Song

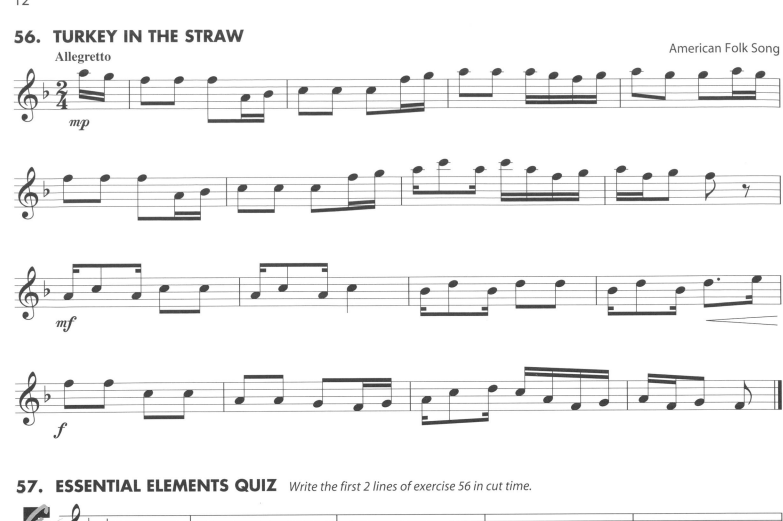

57. ESSENTIAL ELEMENTS QUIZ *Write the first 2 lines of exercise 56 in cut time.*

THEORY

Sixteenth Notes and Rests
in $\frac{6}{8}$, $\frac{3}{8}$, $\frac{9}{8}$, $\frac{12}{8}$

♪ = ½ beat   𝄿 = ½ beat   ♩ = 2 beats   𝄽 = 2 beats
♪ = 1 beat   𝄾 = 1 beat   ♩. = 3 beats   𝄽. = 3 beats

58. RHYTHM RAP

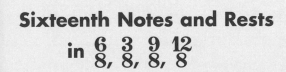

59. SONATINA

D MINOR

60. NATURAL MINOR

61. HARMONIC MINOR

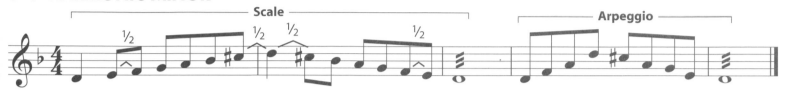

62. COSSACK MARCH

63. SLAVONIC DANCE NO. 2

Antonin Dvořák

64. ESSENTIAL ELEMENTS QUIZ – THE PRETTY GIRL

Irish

A♭ MAJOR

65. SCALE AND ARPEGGIO

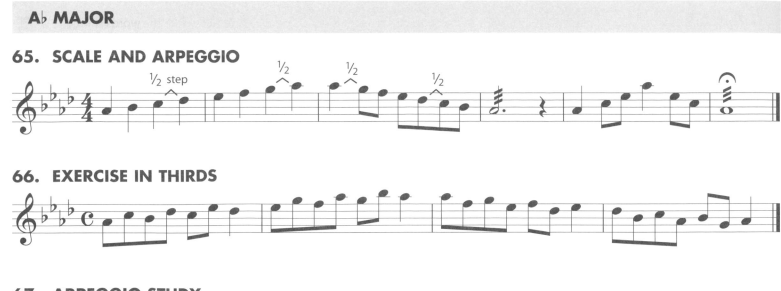

66. EXERCISE IN THIRDS

67. ARPEGGIO STUDY

68. TWO-PART ETUDE

69. CHROMATIC SCALE

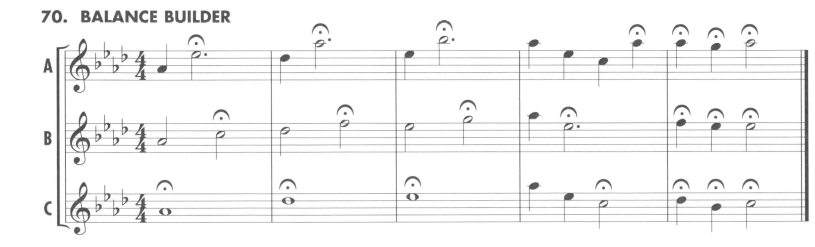

70. BALANCE BUILDER

71. CHORALE

HISTORY

The Star Spangled Banner is the national anthem of the United States of America. Francis Scott Key wrote the words during the 1814 battle at Fort McHenry. He listened to the sounds of the fighting throughout the night while being detained on a ship. At dawn, he saw the American flag still flying over the fort. He was inspired to write these words, which were later set to the melody of a popular English song.

72. THE STAR SPANGLED BANNER

Words by Francis Scott Key
Music by John Stafford Smith

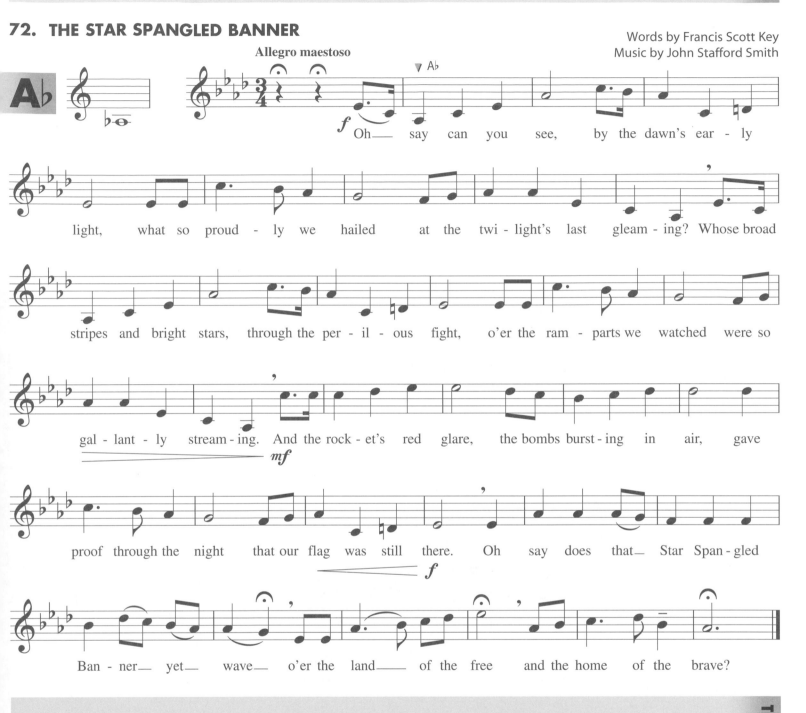

Oh— say can you see, by the dawn's ear - ly light, what so proud - ly we hailed at the twi - light's last gleam - ing? Whose broad stripes and bright stars, through the per - il - ous fight, o'er the ram - parts we watched were so gal - lant - ly stream - ing. And the rock - et's red glare, the bombs burst - ing in air, gave proof through the night that our flag was still there. Oh say does that— Star Span - gled Ban - ner— yet— wave— o'er the land—— of the free and the home of the brave?

THEORY

Dynamics

pp – *pianissimo* (play very softly)   *ff* – *fortissimo* (play very loudly)
Remember to use full breath support to produce the best possible tone and intonation.

73. INTERMEZZO

74. RHYTHM RAP

75. MORNING STAR

Moderato

mf

76. SONATA

Wolfgang Amadeus Mozart

Andante grazioso ◁ *Gracefully*

77. RONDEAU

Jean-Joseph Mouret

Allegro

THEORY

Grace Note ♪   A small note (or notes) which is played on, or slightly before the beat.

78. JULIET'S WALTZ

Charles Gounod

Tempo di valse

mf

F MINOR

79. NATURAL MINOR

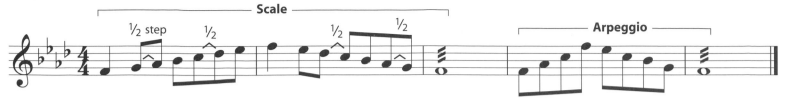

80. HARMONIC MINOR

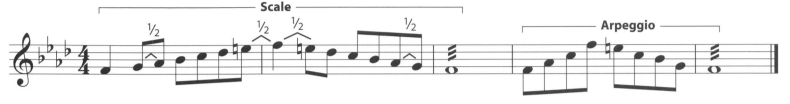

81. SORCERER'S APPRENTICE

Paul Dukas

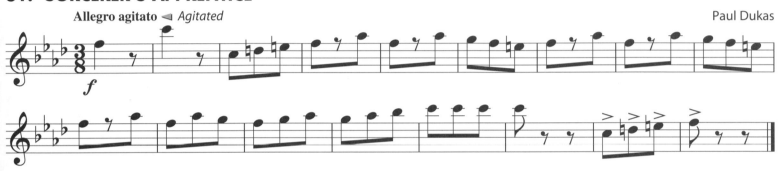

82. I WALK THE ROAD AGAIN

American

83. ESSENTIAL ELEMENTS QUIZ – GREENSLEEVES

English Folk Song

C MAJOR

84. SCALE AND ARPEGGIO

85. EXERCISE IN THIRDS

86. ARPEGGIO STUDY

87. TWO-PART ETUDE

88. CHROMATIC SCALE

△ D♯ (E♭ enharmonic)

89. BALANCE BUILDER

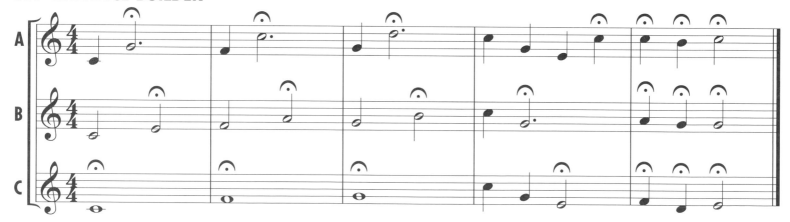

90. CHORALE

Andante

mf

rit.

Black American spirituals originated in the 1700's. As one of the largest categories of true American folk music, these melodies were sung and passed on for generations without being written down. Black and white people worked together to publish the first spiritual collection in 1867, four years after *The Emancipation Proclamation* was signed into law.

91. SIT DOWN, SISTER

Black American Spiritual

92. SPINNING SONG – Duet

Johann Ellmenreich

THEORY

Quarter Note Triplets

Similar to eighth note triplets where 1 beat is divided into 3 equal notes, quarter note triplets divide 2 beats into 3 equal notes.

93. RHYTHM RAP

▼ *1 beat divided into 3 notes.*　　　　　▼ *2 beats divided into 3 notes.*

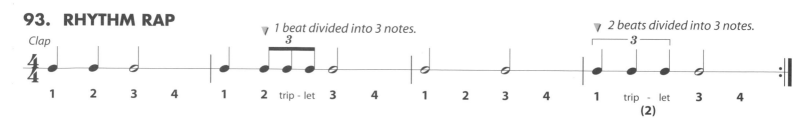

94. THREE FOR TWO

95. SURIRAM'S SONG

Malaysian Folk Song

Allegro

mf

f　　　　　*mf*

HISTORY

Africa is a large continent that is made up of many nations, and **African folk music** is as diverse as its many cultures. Folk songs from any country are expressions of work, love, war, sadness and joy. This song is from Tanzania. The words describe a rabbit hopping and running through a field. Listen to the percussion section play African-sounding drums and rhythms.

96. JIBULI (The Rabbit's Song)

Adapted Tanzanian Folk Song

A MINOR

97. NATURAL MINOR

98. HARMONIC MINOR

△ G♯ (A♭ enharmonic)

THEORY

Meter Changes

Meter changes, or changing time signatures within a section of music, are commonly found in contemporary music. Composers use this technique to create a unique rhythm, pulse, or musical style.

99. TIME ZONES

HISTORY

Important French composers of the late 19th century include **Claude Debussy** (1862–1918), **Gabriel Fauré** (1845–1924), **Erik Satie** (1866–1925), **César Franck** (1822–1890), **Camille Saint-Saëns** (1835–1921), and **Paul Dukas** (1865–1935). Their works continue to have influence on the music of modern day composers. Gabriel Fauré wrote *Pavanne* (originally for orchestra) in 1887, two years before the Eiffel Tower was completed in Paris.

100. PAVANNE

Gabriel Fauré

Db MAJOR

101. SCALE AND ARPEGGIO

102. EXERCISE IN THIRDS

103. ARPEGGIO STUDY

104. TWO-PART ETUDE

105. CHROMATIC SCALE

106. BALANCE BUILDER

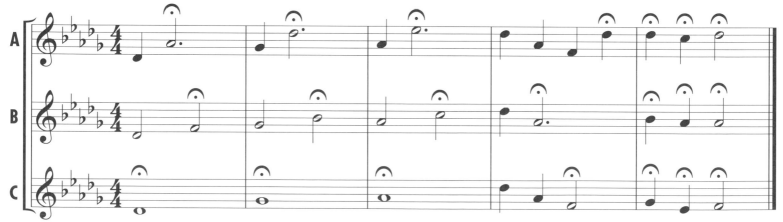

107. CHORALE

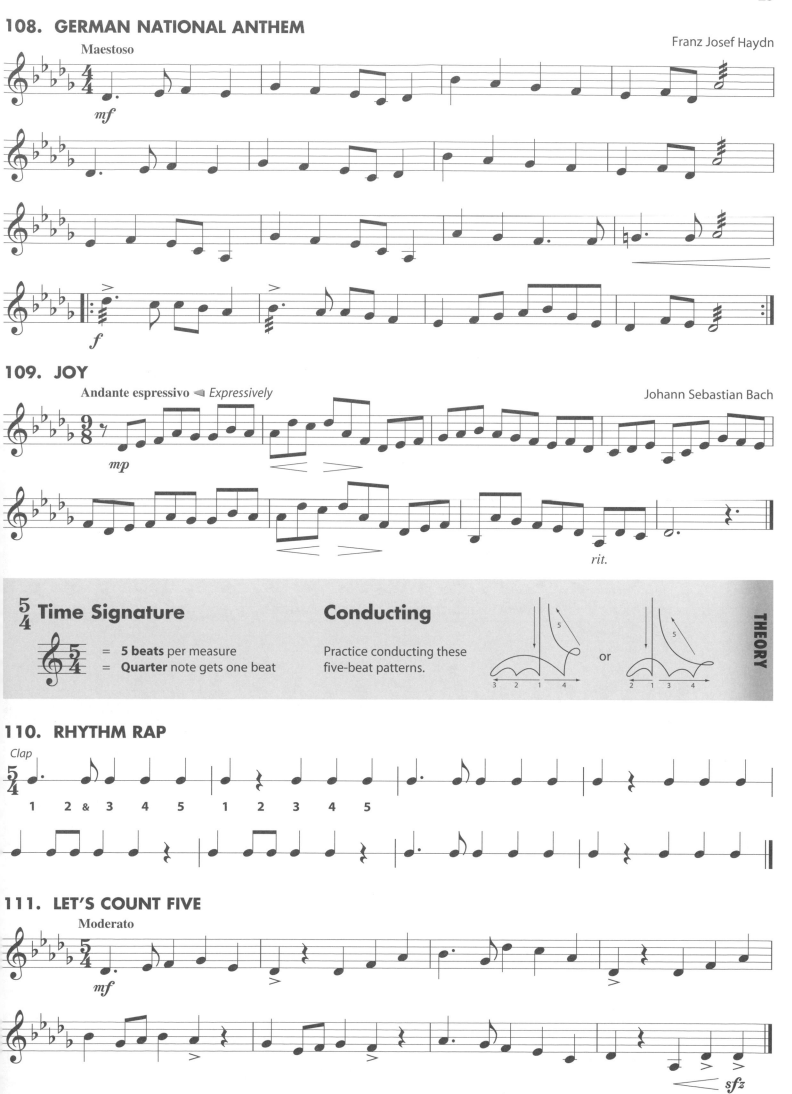

112. SUKURU ITO

Moderato

African Folk Song

mf

113. WATER MUSIC

Allegro maestoso

George Frideric Handel

f

Xylo.
div.

Bells

114. ESSENTIAL TECHNIQUE QUIZ – PICTURES AT AN EXHIBITION

Modeste Mussorgsky

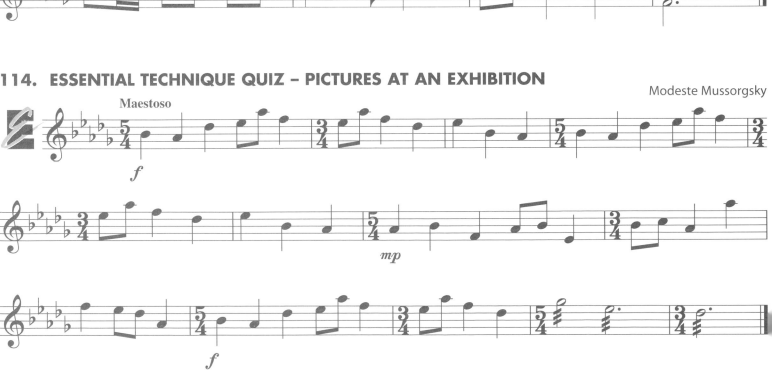

Maestoso

f

mp

f

Bb MINOR

115. NATURAL MINOR

116. HARMONIC MINOR

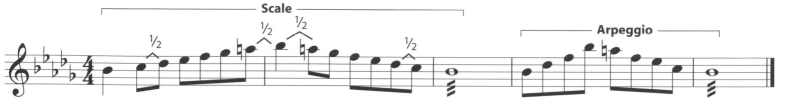

Ostinato   A clear and distinct musical phrase that is repeated persistently.

THEORY

British composer **Gustav Holst** (1874–1934) is one of the most widely played composers for concert band today. Many of his compositions, including his familiar military suites, are based on tuneful English folk songs. His most famous work for orchestra, *The Planets (1916)*, has seven movements—one written for each known planet, excluding Earth. At this time, Pluto was undiscovered.

HISTORY

117. MARS – Duet/Trio

Gustav Holst

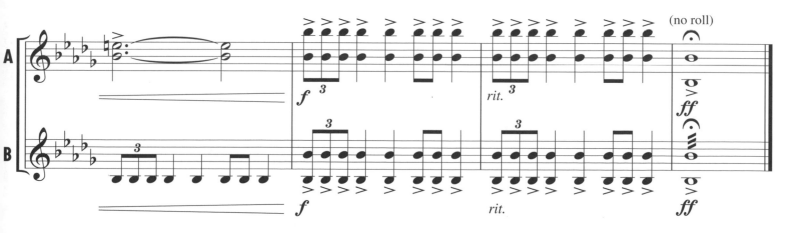

G MAJOR

118. SCALE AND ARPEGGIO

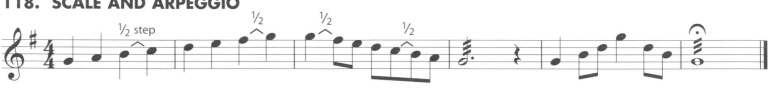

119. EXERCISE IN THIRDS

120. ARPEGGIO STUDY

121. TWO-PART ETUDE

122. CHROMATIC SCALE

123. BALANCE BUILDER

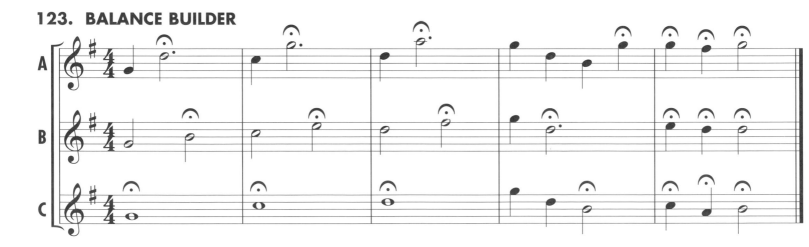

124. CHORALE

Norwegian composer **Edvard Grieg** (1843–1907) based much of his music on the folk songs and dances of Norway. During the late 19th century, composers often used melodies from their native land. This trend is called **nationalism**. Russian **Modeste Mussorgsky** (1839–1881), Czech **Antonin Dvořák** (1841–1904), and Englishman **Sir Edward Elgar** (1857–1934) are other famous composers whose music was influenced by nationalism.

125. NORWEGIAN DANCE

126. FRENCH NATIONAL ANTHEM (LA MARSEILLAISE)

Music written during the **Renaissance Period (1430–1600)** was often upbeat and dance-like. *Wolsey's Wilde* was originally written for the lute, an ancestor to the guitar and the most popular instrument of the Renaissance era. Modern day concert band composer Gordon Jacob used this popular song in his *William Byrd Suite,* written as a tribute to English composer William Byrd (1543–1623).

127. WOLSEY'S WILDE

E MINOR

128. NATURAL MINOR

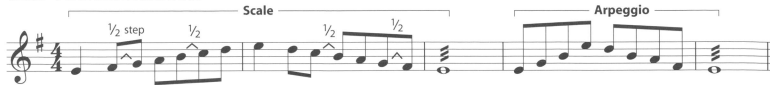

129. HARMONIC MINOR

130. SONG OF THE SHAKUHACHI

Japanese Folk Song

131. POLOVETZIAN DANCES

Alexander Borodin

D MAJOR

132. SCALE AND ARPEGGIO

133. EXERCISE IN THIRDS

134. ARPEGGIO STUDY

135. TWO-PART ETUDE

136. CHORALE

B MINOR

137. NATURAL MINOR

138. HARMONIC MINOR

Latin American Music combines the folk music from South and Central America, the Carribean Islands, American Indian, Spanish, and Portuguese cultures. Melodies are often accompanied by drums, maracas, and claves. Latin American music continues to influence jazz, classical, and popular styles of music. *Cielito Lindo* is a Latin American love song.

139. CIELITO LINDO

C. Fernandez

Tchaikovsky, along with Wagner, Brahms, Mendelssohn, and Chopin, helped define the musical era known as the **Romantic Period (1825–1900)**. The "symphonic tone poem" from this period continues to be one of the most popular musical forms performed by orchestras and bands today.

140. WALTZ IN FIVE (from SYMPHONY NO. 6)

Peter I. Tchaikovsky

141. THE YOUNG CHEVALIER

Scottish

Gb MAJOR

142. SCALE AND ARPEGGIO

143. EXERCISE IN THIRDS

144. ARPEGGIO STUDY

145. TWO-PART ETUDE

146. CHORALE

Eb MINOR

147. NATURAL MINOR

148. HARMONIC MINOR

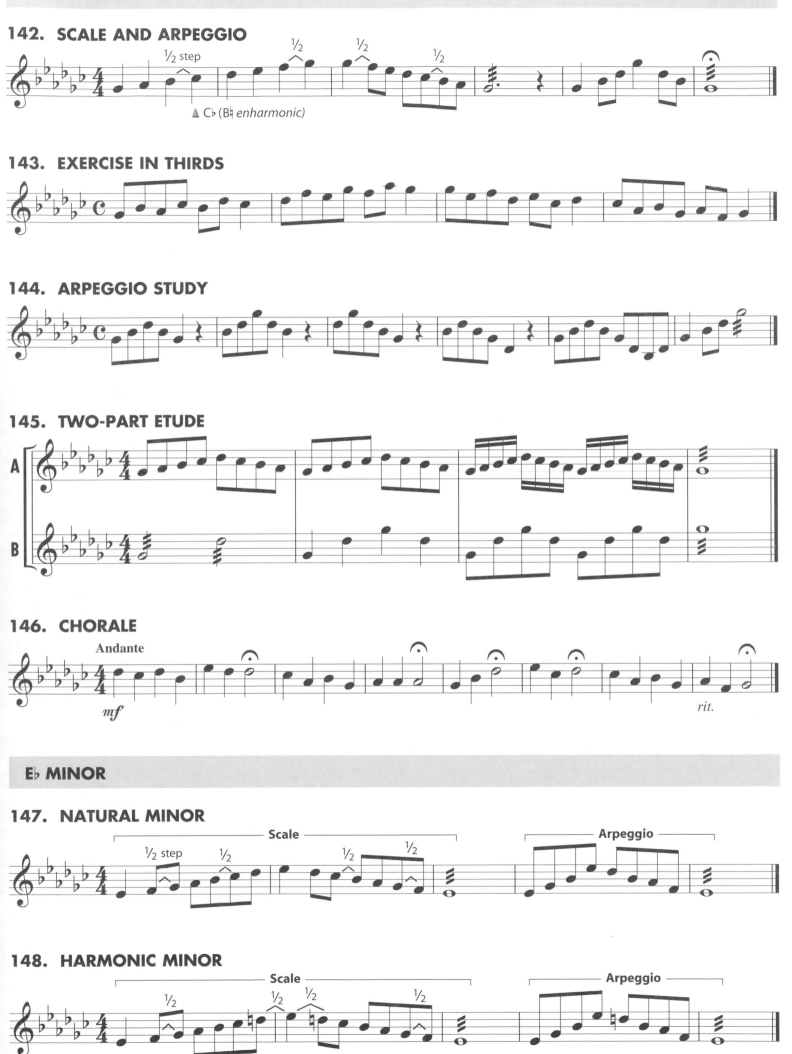

INDIVIDUAL STUDY – Keyboard Percussion

Exercises 149–157 provide an introduction to four mallet technique. Ideally, they should be practiced on a marimba. However, they are written to fit the range of a concert xylophone.

INDIVIDUAL STUDY – Keyboard Percussion

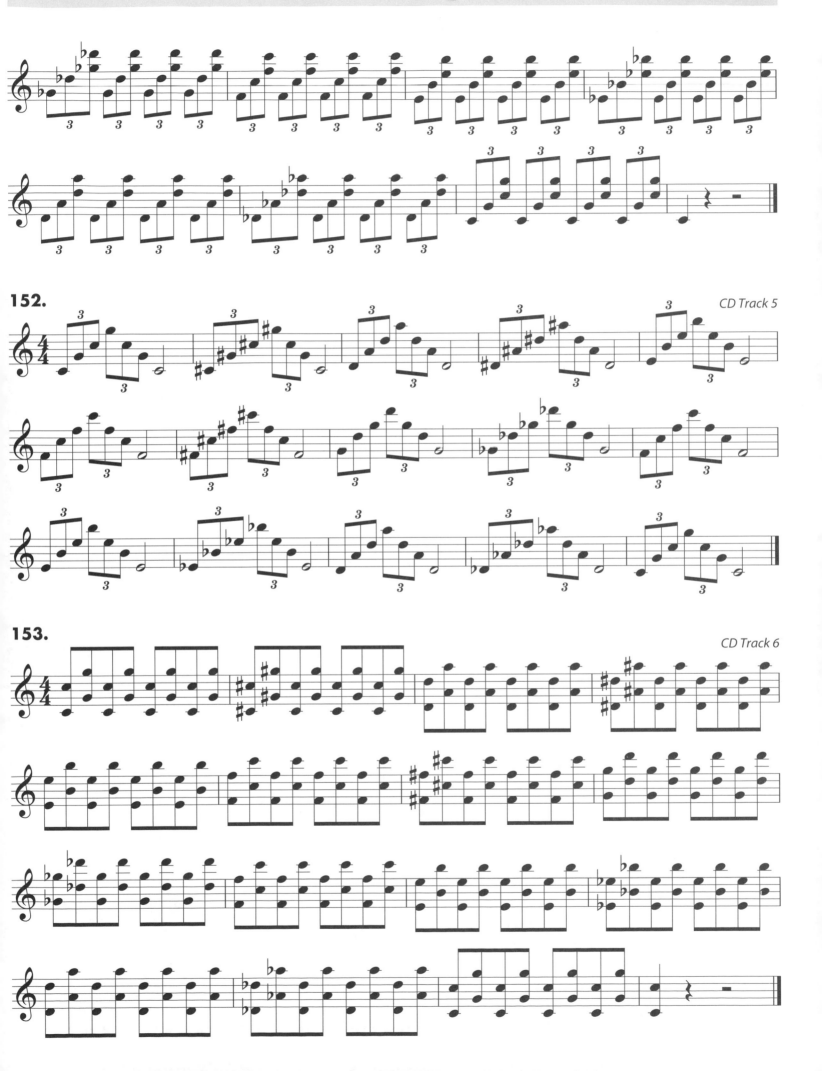

INDIVIDUAL STUDY – Keyboard Percussion

154.

CD Track 7

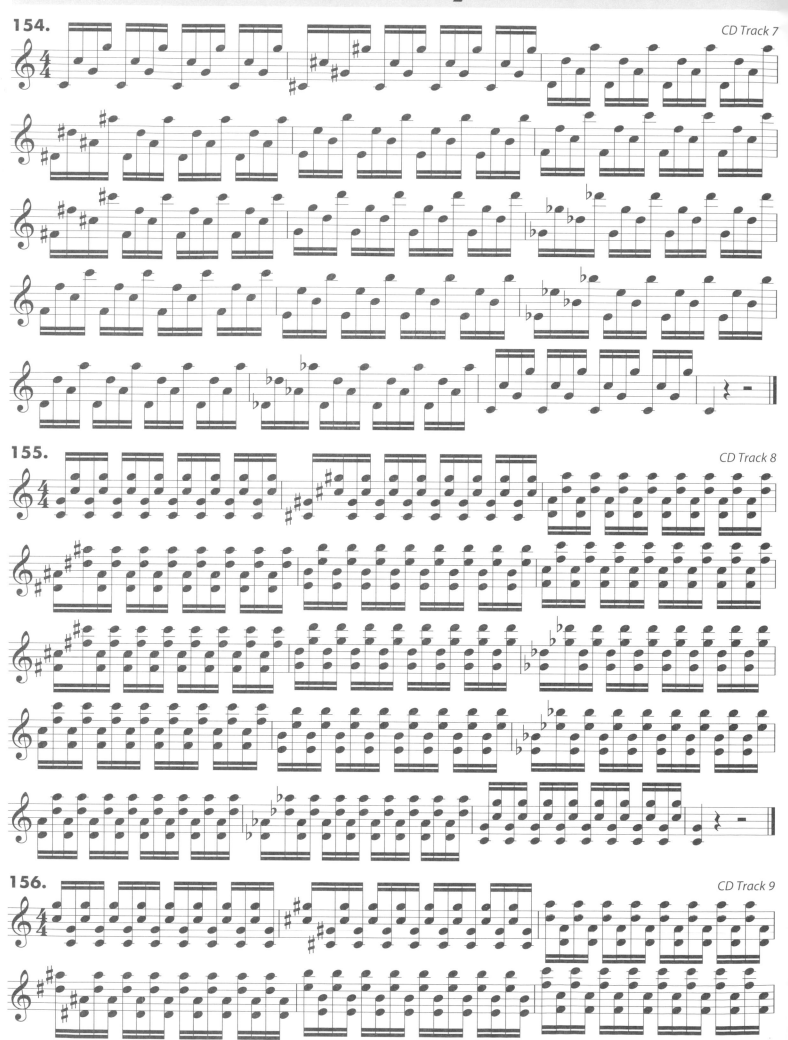

155.

CD Track 8

156.

CD Track 9

INDIVIDUAL STUDY – Keyboard Percussion

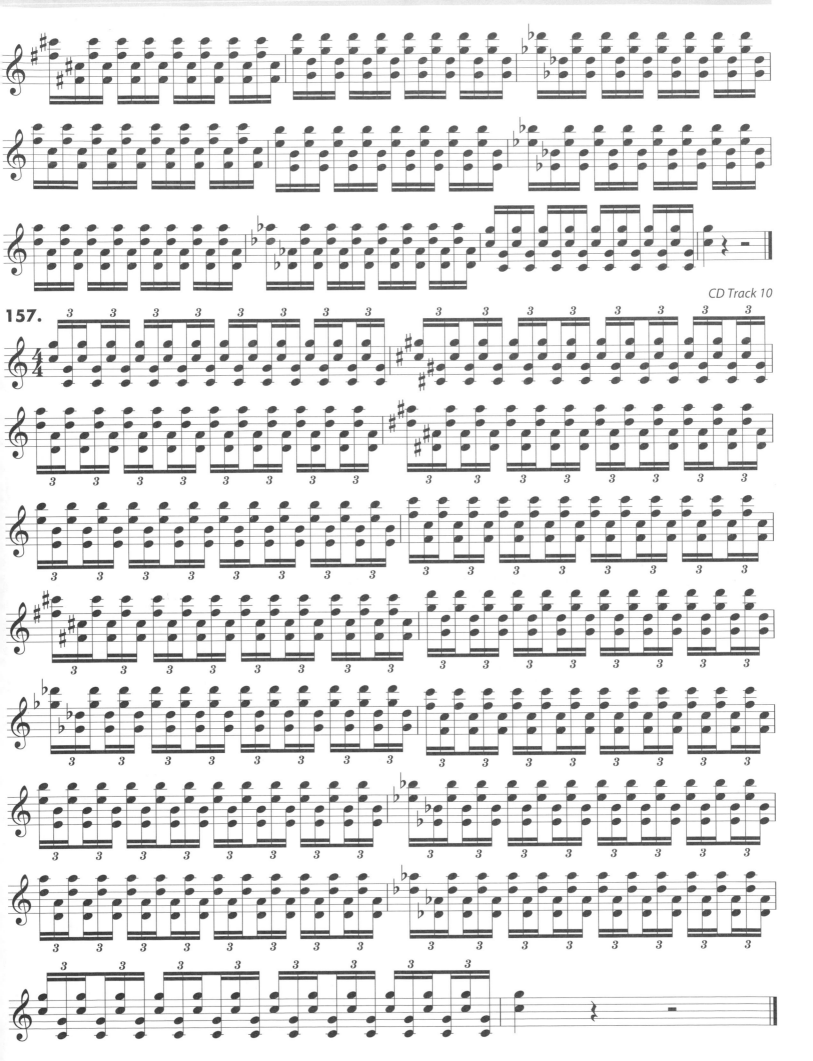

CD Track 10

157.

READING SKILL BUILDERS

158. READING SKILL BUILDER NO. 1

CD Track 11

159. READING SKILL BUILDER NO. 2

CD Track 12

160. READING SKILL BUILDER NO. 3

CD Track 13

161. READING SKILL BUILDER NO. 4

CD Track 14

162. READING SKILL BUILDER NO. 5

CD Track 15

READING SKILL BUILDERS

163. READING SKILL BUILDER NO. 6

CD Track 16

164. READING SKILL BUILDER NO. 7

CD Track 17

165. READING SKILL BUILDER NO. 8

CD Track 18

Fine

D.C. al Fine

166. READING SKILL BUILDER NO. 9

CD Track 19

167. CHORALE (Prelude from Hansel and Gretel) *CD Track 20*

Engelbert Humperdinck
Arr. by John Higgins

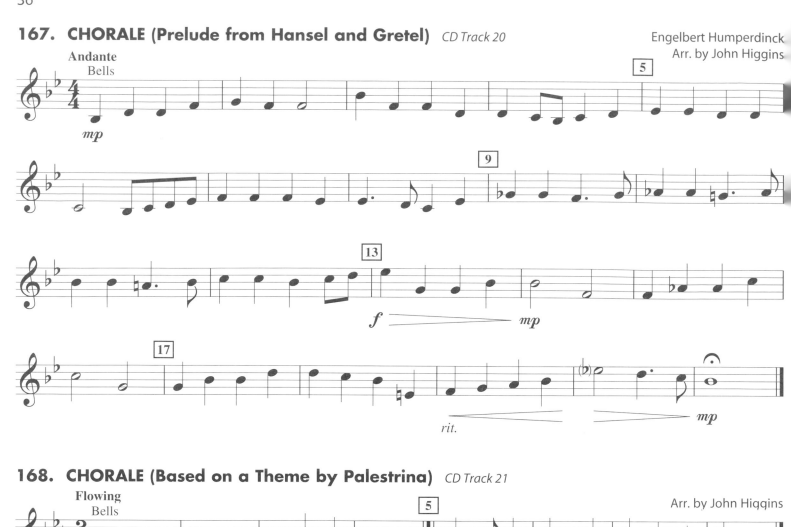

168. CHORALE (Based on a Theme by Palestrina) *CD Track 21*

Arr. by John Higgins

169. CHORALE (Based on a Theme by J. S. Bach) *CD Track 22*

Arr. by John Higgins

170. CHORALE (Based on a Theme by Tchaikovsky) *CD Track 23*

Broadly
Bells
Arr. by John Higgins

mp

rall.

171. CHORALE (Erhalt Uns In Der Wahrheit) *CD Track 24*

Johann Sebastian Bach
Arr. by John Higgins

Andante
Bells

mf

rit.

172. CHORALE (Navy Hymn) *CD Track 25*

John Dykes
Arr. by John Higgins

Andante
Bells

mp

p

cresc.

mf rall.

173. CHORALE (Prelude) *CD Track 26*

Frederic Chopin
Arr. by John Higgins

Adagio
Bells

f

p

RHYTHM STUDIES

CD Tracks 27–28

RHYTHM STUDIES

CD Tracks 37–38

CD Tracks 39–40

CD Tracks 41–42

CD Tracks 43–44

CD Tracks 45–46

THE BASICS OF JAZZ STYLE

from Essential Elements for Jazz Ensemble

Accenting "2 and 4"

For most traditional music the important beats in 4/4 time are 1 and 3. In jazz, however, the emphasis is usually on beats 2 and 4. Emphasizing "2 and 4" gives the music a jazz feeling.

174. ACCENTING 2 AND 4 *CD Track 47*

Jazz Articulations

These are the four basic articulations in jazz.

| Tenuto (full value) | Staccato (short, unaccented) | Long Accent (full value, accented) | Roof Top Accent (short, accented) |

Swing 8th Notes Sound Different Than They Look

In swing, the 2nd 8th note of each beat is actually played like the last third of a triplet, and slightly accented. 8th notes in swing style are usually played legato.

175. SWING 8TH NOTES *CD Track 48*

Quarter Notes

Quarter notes in swing style are usually played detached (staccato) with accents on beats 2 and 4.

176. QUARTERS AND 8THS *CD Track 49*

177. RUNNIN' AROUND *CD Track 50*

Syncopation in Jazz

When beats are played early (anticipated) or played late (delayed), the music becomes syncopated. Syncopation makes the music sound "jazzy."

178. WHEN THE SAINTS GO MARCHING IN – Without Syncopation *CD Track 51*

James Black and Katherine Purvis

179. WHEN THE SAINTS GO MARCHING IN – With Syncopation *CD Track 52*

"Jazzin' Up" the Melody by Adding Rhythms

Adding rhythms to a melody is another easy way to improvise in a jazz style. Start by filling out long notes with repeated 8th and quarter notes. Remember to swing the 8th notes (play legato and give the upbeats an accent).

180. "JAZZIN' UP" JINGLE BELLS *CD Track 53*

Original Melody

J. Pierpont

Jazzed Up Melody (rhythms added)

MAKE UP YOUR OWN (IMPROVISE) *CD Track 54*

181. LONDON BRIDGE *Complete the melody in your own "jazzed up" way. Use only the notes shown in parentheses. Slashes on the staff indicate when to improvise.*

Original Melody

Jazzed Up Melody

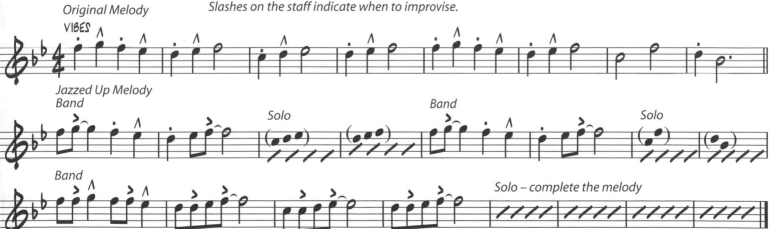

THEORY

Major Scales

Play major scales as part of your daily practice routine. Play all octaves, keys and arpeggios at various dynamic levels and tempos. Keep a steady pulse. If you perform any of these exercises with the full band, you may hear different articulation patterns, such as:

A.   **B.**   **C.**

182. B♭ MAJOR

CD Track 55

183. E♭ MAJOR

CD Track 56

184. F MAJOR

CD Track 57

185. C MAJOR

CD Track 58

186. A♭ MAJOR

CD Track 59

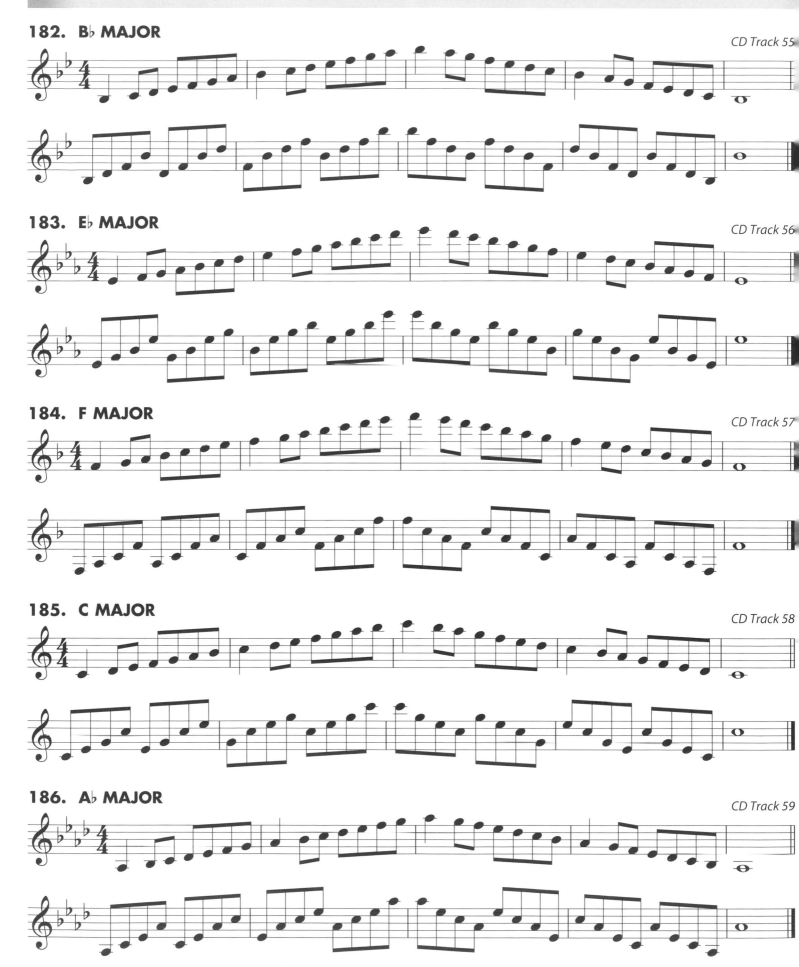

187. D♭ MAJOR

CD Track 60

188. G MAJOR

CD Track 61

189. D MAJOR

CD Track 62

190. A MAJOR

CD Track 63

191. G♭ MAJOR

CD Track 64

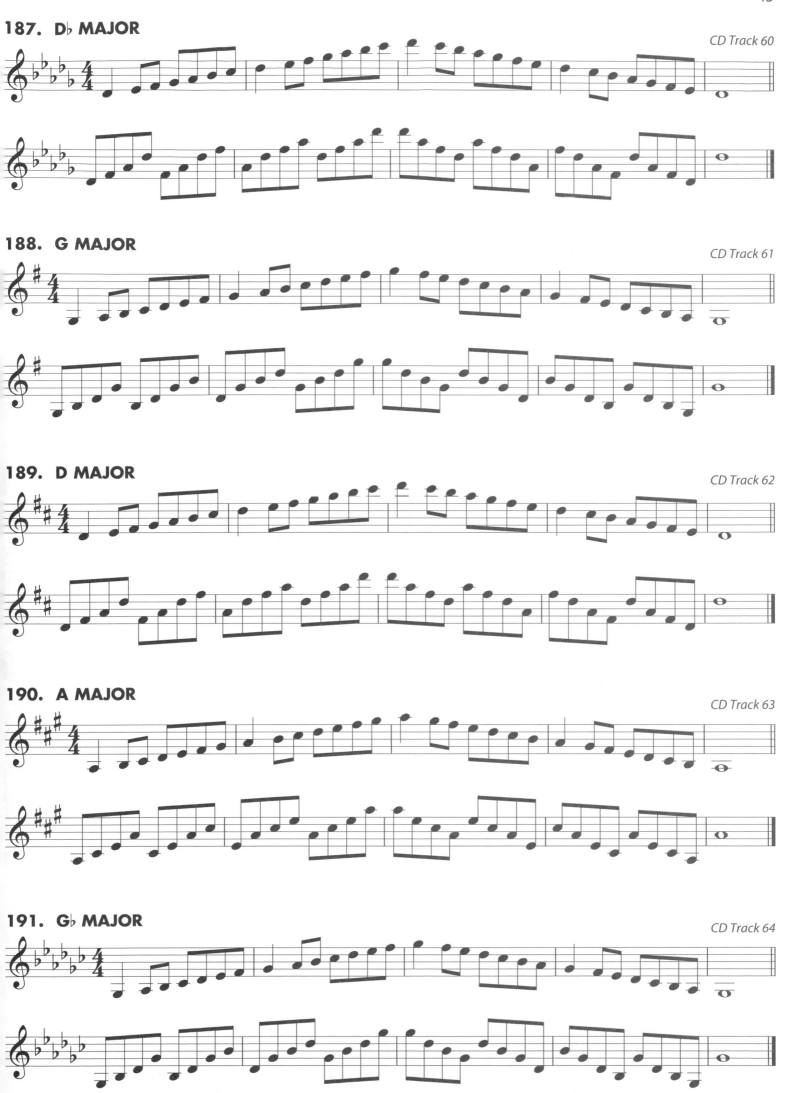

THEORY

Minor Scales

Play minor scales as part of your daily practice routine. Play all octaves, all three forms and the arpeggios at various dynamic levels and tempos. Keep a steady pulse. If you perform these exercises with the full band, you may hear different articulation patterns, such as:

192. D MINOR SCALE

CD Track 65

193. G MINOR SCALE

CD Track 66

194. C MINOR SCALE

CD Track 67

195. F MINOR SCALE

CD Track 68

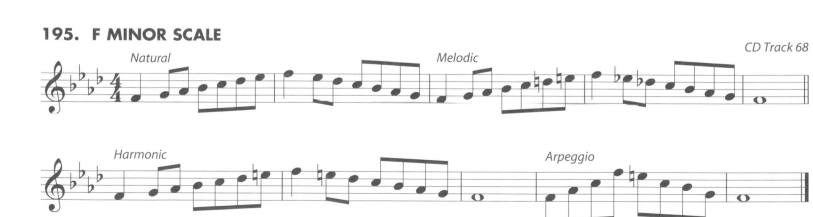

SPECIAL EXERCISES KEYBOARD PERCUSSION

INTERVALS

OCTAVES

ARPEGGIO ENCOUNTER NO. 1

ARPEGGIO ENCOUNTER NO. 2

KEYBOARD PERCUSSION INSTRUMENTS

Each keyboard percussion instrument has a unique sound because of the materials used to create the instrument. Ranges may differ with some models of instruments.

Instrument Care Reminders

- Cover all percussion instruments when they are not being used.
- Put mallets away in a storage area. Keep the percussion section neat!
- Mallets are the only things which should be placed on your instrument. NEVER put or allow others to put objects on any percussion instrument.

BELLS (Orchestra Bells)

- Bars – metal alloy or steel
- Mallets – lexan (hard plastic), brass or hard rubber
- Range – 2 1/2 octaves
- Sounds 2 octaves higher than written

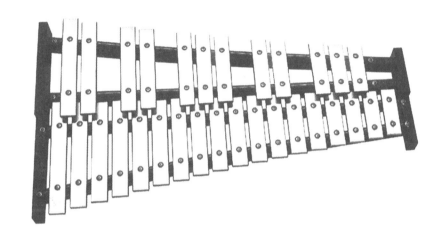

XYLOPHONE

- Bars – wooden or synthetic
- Mallets – hard rubber
- Range – 3 1/2 octaves
- Sounds 1 octave higher than written

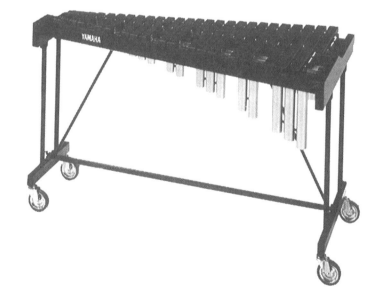

MARIMBA

- Bars – wooden (wider than xylophone bars) Resonating tube located below each bar
- Mallets – soft to medium rubber or yarn covered
- Range – 4 1/3 octaves (reads bass and treble clefs)
- Sounding pitch is the same as written pitch

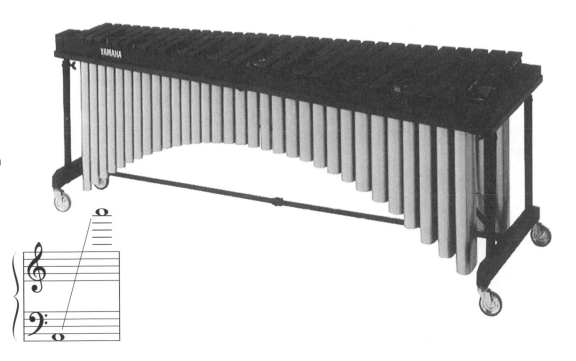

VIBRAPHONE

- Bars – metal alloy or aluminum Resonating tubes located below each bar Adjustable electric fans in each resonator create "vibrato" effect
- Mallets – yarn covered
- Range – 3 octaves
- Sounding pitch is the same as written pitch

CHIMES

- Bars – metal tubes
- Mallets – plastic, rawhide or wooden
- Range – 1 1/2 octaves
- Sounding pitch is the same as written pitch

Instruments and photos courtesy of Yamaha Corporation of America, Band and Orchestral Division

REFERENCE INDEX

Definitions (pg.)

Allegro Agitato   17
Allegro Marziale   27
Allegro Vivo   13
Andante Espressivo   23
Andante Grazioso   16
Animato   27
D.C. al Coda   28
D.S. al Coda   28
Divisi *(div.)*   2
Energetico   25
5/4   23
Fortissimo (*ff*)   15
Giocoso   11
Grace Note   16
Lento   8
Lento Mysterioso   9
Maestoso   3
Meter Changes   21
Minor Keys   5
Molto Rit.   8
9/8   4
Ostinato   25
Quarter Note Triplets   20
Pianissimo (*pp*)   15
16th Notes and Rests
   in 6/8, 3/8, 9/8, 12/8   12
Tempo Di Valse   7
3/8   4
Triplets with Rests   11
12/8   8
Unison *(a2)*   2

Composers

JOHANN SEBASTIAN BACH
• Joy   23

ALEXANDER BORODIN
• Polovetzian Dances   28

CLAUDE DEBUSSY
• The Little Child   11

PAUL DUKAS
• Sorcerer's Apprentice   17

ANTONIN DVORÁK
• Slavonic Dance No. 2   13

JOHANN ELLMENREICH
• Spinning Song   19

GABRIEL FAURÉ
• Pavanne   21

CHARLES GOUNOD
• Juliet's Waltz   16

EDVARD GRIEG
• Norwegian Dance   27

GEORGE FRIDERIC HANDEL
• Hallelujah Chorus   3
• Sound An Alarm   3
• Water Music   24

FRANZ JOSEF HAYDN
• German National Anthem   23

GUSTAV HOLST
• Mars   25

JEAN-JOSEPH MOURET
• Rondeau   16

WOLFGANG AMADEUS MOZART
• Sonata   16

MODESTE MUSSORGSKY
• Great Gate of Kiev   3
• Pictures at an Exhibition   24

JOHANN STRAUSS JR.
• Adele's Song   7

PETER I. TCHAIKOVSKY
• Waltz in Five
   (from Symphony No. 6)   30

World Music

AFRICAN
• Jibuli   20
• Sukuru Ito   24

AMERICAN
• Children's Shoes   3
• I Walk the Road Again   17
• The Keel Row   7
• Keepin' Secrets   7
• Sit Down, Sister   19
• Star Spangled Banner   15
• Turkey in the Straw   12

AUSTRALIAN
• Australian Folk Song   5

ENGLISH
• Greensleeves   17
• Molly Bann   4
• Wolsey's Wilde   27

FRENCH
• Pat-A-Pan   5
• French National Anthem   27

IRISH
• The Pretty Girl   13

JAPANESE
• Song of the Shakuhachi   28

LATIN AMERICAN
• Cielito Lindo   30

MALAYSIAN
• Suriram's Song   20

NATIVE AMERICAN INDIAN
• Song of the Weeping Spirit   9

RUSSIAN
• The Sledgehammer Song   5

SCOTTISH
• Scottish Legend   9
• The Young Chevalier   30

REFERENCE INDEX FOR PERCUSSION

Definitions (pg.)*

These page numbers refer to the first section (percussion) of this book.

Notes

Notes

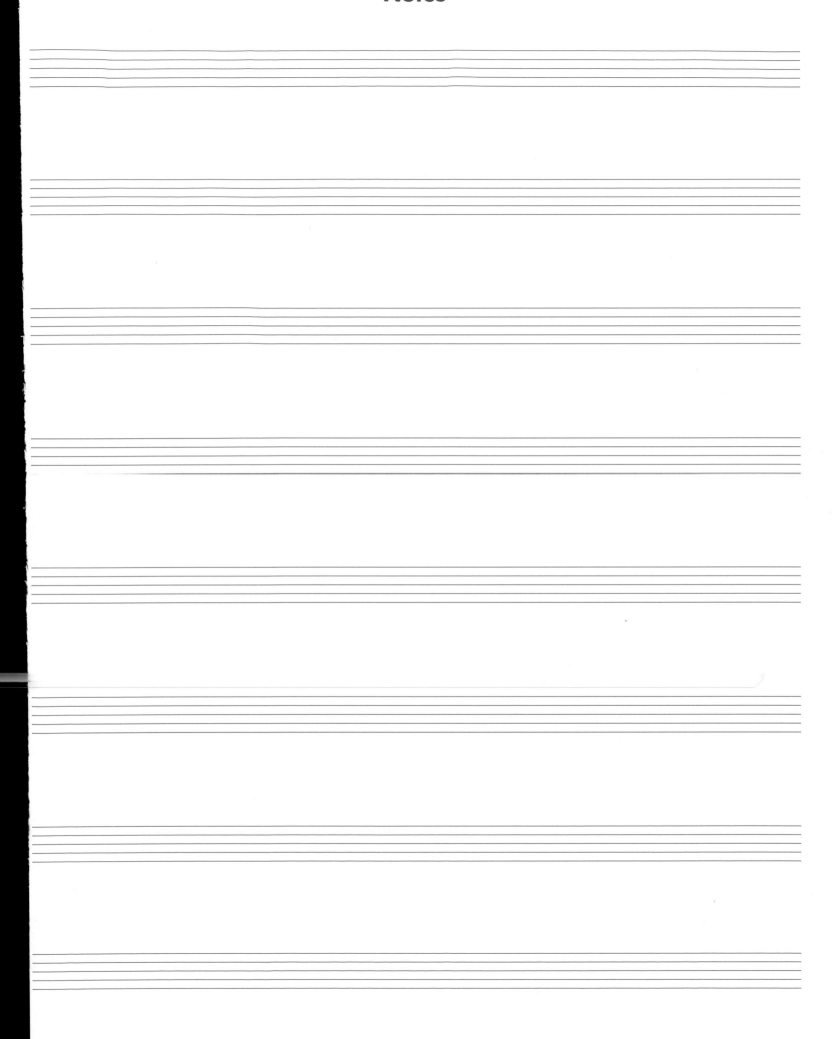

Notes